Praise for

Through God's grace and compassion, a soul was given an opportunity to be reborn. Through her strength, she has persevered and used her experience to encourage others to continue the fight against human trafficking. I'm so honored to now be her friend.

DETECTIVE KIM CLARK
Crimes Against Children Unit
Waco Police Department

Powerful tool, provides direction and courage to getting out of "The Life."

SGT. BYRON FASSETT
Ret. Dallas PD

Julia is a living testimony that one does not have to be defined by their past experiences or other people. Her story will bring hope to the voiceless and will inspire others that they too are worthy of change.

ALLISON FRANKLIN
Survivor Leader/Consultant
Policy Fellow
Texas Criminal Justice Coalition

SURVIVING "THE LIFE"

SURVIVING
"THE LIFE"

HOW I OVERCAME

SEX TRAFFICKING

By Julia Walsh
with Natalie Garnett MacDonald

ISBN 978-0-692-03969-4
First edition printed 2018 in the United States of America

Cover photograph by Sweet Magnolia Photography
Interior photographs courtesy of the author

Antioch Community Church dba UnBound
505 N 20th Street
Waco, Texas 76707
UnBoundnow.org

18 19 20 21 22   5 4 3 2 1

Human trafficking is "the recruitment, harboring, transportation, provision, or obtaining of a person for labor or services, through the use of *force, fraud, or coercion* for the purpose of subjection to involuntary servitude, peonage, debt bondage, or slavery." Sex trafficking is *"a commercial sex act* induced by **force, fraud, or coercion**, or in which the person induced to perform such act has **not attained 18 years of age**."

The Trafficking Victims Protection Act, 2000

This crime is happening to men, women, and children around the world and in our communities, every day.

If you suspect human trafficking or believe you may be a victim, call the National Human Trafficking Hotline at 1-888-373-7888 or text "INFO" or "BEFREE" to 233733. In an emergency, always call 911. Additional steps to identify human trafficking or seek help can be found at the back of this book.

The names and locations involved in Julia's years of trafficking have been changed for her protection. All stories are told from Julia's perspective.

TABLE OF CONTENTS

FOREWORD

Domestic Sex Trafficking. I'm amazed at how, in 2018, the term *Domestic Sex Trafficking* is still foreign to so many. While hundreds of thousands of American men, women and children are sold for sex in the streets, the clubs, and on the Internet, hundreds of thousands of Americans remain uneducated about the issue. So many still believe sex trafficking happens in other countries or in big cities but turn a blind eye to the victims in their own backyards. Victims are hidden in plain sight, and we pass by them daily as we live our lives in freedom.

Julia Walsh was one such victim. She was held against her will, forced to do unimaginable things, abused, and tortured. She was beaten down and beaten up. Her traffickers each tried to kill the deepest parts of her soul but could not crush her spirit. Julia's journey from orphanages to adoption to trafficking to redemption to thriving is a beautiful one, an inspirational one. She has lost much in her young life, and through her journey she has gained so much! She has learned her worth and her value. She has found her voice. She has become a voice for the voiceless, educating those she meets about the truth of sex trafficking in America. She has overcome the stigma and shame, and has stepped into the role of mentor, advocate, and survivor leader. Julia's story is heart-breaking and gut-wrenching, but Julia's story is also beautiful and filled with healing and redemption. Julia Walsh is more than a "Survivor." She is more than any labels or titles or accolades.

You will be blessed and inspired as you get a glimpse into her journey. If you are currently being exploited, I believe you will find the strength to find help as you read of her bravery. If you are in the midst of your healing journey, I believe you will find the courage to go one more day. If you are one who has not seen the atrocities in your own backyard, I believe you will have knowledge and be unable to look the other way. If you are in law enforcement, I believe you will be better equipped to help victims you encounter. No matter who you are, I believe you will understand more and will be inspired by Julia and this book.

BOBBIE MARK
Director of Client Care
Redeemed Ministries

REDEEMED

Redeemed Ministries is one of the few organizations in the nation operating a long-term residential program dedicated exclusively to the trauma-informed care of adult domestic victims of sex trafficking. Redeemed owns and operates an 8-bed restoration house in the Houston area for women rescued from their slavery. For more information, visit **RedeemedMinistries.com**.

PREFACE

Dear Reader,

My name is Julia Walsh, and I am a survivor of sex trafficking. I share my story so others may know that not only can you survive sex trafficking, but you can have a bright and successful future. I also tell this story so that others, such as the general public, law enforcement officers, health professionals, and other service providers, may gain awareness of the sex trafficking industry and the insidious ways it entraps victims.

I could fill a hundred chapters with details large and small about my childhood, my experiences in "The Life," and my life since then, but I have kept my narrative compact to focus on sharing what I think is most important for you to know.

Some of you may see yourself in my story and relate to the feelings I've described. Maybe you have been or are still in "The Life." I want to share what I have been xvi | SURVIVING "THE LIFE"

through with the desire that it will inspire you and give you a glimmer of hope like the one shared with me. I tell you my story to help you see that although what you've been through (or are going through right now) is real and scary, there is a way to get out and stay out. I pray this book will give you hope and courage to step out toward your own freedom. I hope you can learn to separate who you are from what's been done to you. I hope you know you are valuable enough to deserve a real life, not just a life of survival. Please know that there are people out there who will help and protect you. You are not alone and are never forgotten. Hold onto hope. This book is for you.

Others of you may be shocked by what you read in this book. Although I know you've experienced your own pain and challenges, this story may be foreign to you. I know it is hard to read, but I hope it will help you develop a greater compassion for women, men, and children forced into the "commercial sex industry" and human trafficking. I hope you're able to move past your shock into compassion and on to action to be involved in fighting "human trafficking" and helping victims. You have a very important part to play.

As you read, you'll hear about friends, police, and others who failed me. But the story doesn't end there. Keep reading, and you'll see these same people helped set me free.

Wherever you're coming from, thank you for choosing to enter into the pain of my story. I hope you'll also join me in the great hope I have for my own future and for others who have survived similar experiences.

With Hope,
Julia

ACKNOWLEDGMENTS

There are so many people to thank and so many to whom I could dedicate this book.

I want to thank my Aunt Celia and my mom for their support and thoughtful contributions in helping me with this book.

Thanks to my dad, my Uncle Joe, my Gran and Fa, Paula Shepherd, Allison Brooks, Suzanne Rowntree, and all my family and friends for providing support and encouragement through the transition into my new life.

Thank you to the Lubbock Vice Unit, in particular Detective Curtis Fish and Corporal Billingsley; also, Waco Detective Kim Clark and Sergeant Greg Dickerman for seeing beyond my hardened exterior to the girl hidden inside.

I want to thank the UnBound Waco team, including Natalie Garnett and Susan Peters, for their love and support in continuing to make a way for me. Natalie has tirelessly dedicated herself to helping me put my thoughts to paper and encouraged me to stay strong throughout this writing process. Susan has been such an amazing advocate and continues to connect me with available resources and wonderful opportunities.

Thank you to UnBound Fort Worth Executive Director Stephanie Byrd for your love and encouragement in supporting me as I wrote this book.

I want to thank Redeemed Ministries, especially Bobbie and Dennis Mark, for accepting me with all of my trauma scars and open wounds. Thank you for helping me heal, unconditionally loving me in a tender way I've never known and showing me how to grow into a strong survivor.

Thank you to Voice of Hope, including Kim Stark and Jaime Wheeler, for meeting me at my worst and being a beacon of hope during the tumultuous times when I was navigating between "The Life" and my life as a survivor.

Thank you to Karla Clanton for leading such an amazing support group and for your sweet words of encouragement to both me and my family.

Thank you to Phoenix Charities and Traci Mann for helping me learn that my past does not define me and for giving me a clean slate to write my story.

Thank you to New Friends New Life, including Kara Christensen, for your friendship and guidance navigating life's hurdles in independent living. Your smile and laughter kept me going on so many occasions.

Thank you to Mosaic, including Aroonvan, for your wisdom and pure dedication in helping meet my needs as a new survivor. You cheered me on as I began my journey of healing.

Thank you to Alan Schonborn and Andrea Sparks, from the Child Sex Trafficking Team of the Office of Governor Greg Abbott, for their friendships and encouragement for me to be passionate and stay strong and for their help in building my self-confidence and courage in helping others.

Thank you to Hannah Rivard and Wayne Menzies from the Fort Worth Police Department Human Trafficking Unit for your friendship and passion to hear and value a survivor's perspective in your work. Your stories and laughter bring hope and smiles to me, especially on the tough days.

Thank you to my Survivor Leader friends for your unconditional love and continued loyal support throughout my journey.

I wrote the following the first time I publicly shared my story, seeking to highlight each of the advocacy agencies that have helped me along the way. It still captures how I feel today:

> And finally, thank God. I have been **UnBound** from slavery, renewing my inner strengths and building character. Like a **Phoenix**, I have risen from the ashes of my past traumas, finding my inner strength and beauty. I have been **EmPowered**. I have found my **Voice of Hope**, allowing me to learn who I am, allowing me to advocate for myself as well as for other victims and survivors who have been silenced. I have been generously offered **New Friends** and a **New Life** through all the wonderful advocates and the resources they have offered me. Thanks to all law enforcement, family, and friends who have walked with me every step of the way, I am finally able to both see and to show others that the broken pieces of my shattered life can and are in the process of being mended, molding my traumas and my victories into a beautiful **Mosaic** that tells a story, even more beautiful and powerful than had ever been before. And most importantly, I have been mercifully **Redeemed** from past traumas and choices, allowing my heart and soul the freedom to experience God's love, learn forgiveness, and discover true healing.

> You fought for my freedom when I could not. You saved my life. Thank you.

JULIA'S VOCABULARY LIST

Definitions gathered from Julia's experience, Shared Hope International and Lighthouse for Life

A

Automatic

The victim's *automatic* routine when her pimp is out of town, in jail, or otherwise not in direct contact with those he is prostituting. Victims are expected to comply with the rules and often do so out of fear of punishment or because they have been psychologically manipulated into a sense of loyalty or love. All money generated on *automatic* is turned over to the pimp.

B

Bottom

A female appointed by the trafficker/pimp to help instruct victims, collect money, book hotel rooms, and post ads.

Boyfriending

A method of recruitment into "The Life" by posing as a boyfriend instead of a pimp, using romance and affection to gain the loyalty of a victim.

Branding

A tattoo or carving on a victim that indicates ownership by a trafficker/pimp/gang.

Break a Bitch

To give all one's earnings to a trafficker/pimp after each "date."

Buyer (client, date, John, trick)

Terms used for a person purchasing sex. In some cases, this person can also be convicted for human trafficking.

C

Caught A Case

Getting arrested and charged with a crime.

Circuit

A series of cities or states among which victims are moved while being trafficked.

Coercion

"Threats or perceived threats of serious harm to or physical constraints against a person; a scheme intended to cause a person to believe that failure to perform will result in serious harm to or physical restraint against any person." –Federal Law 22 U.S.C 7102 (3)

D

Daddy
The term a pimp will often require his victim to call him.

Date (service)
Servicing a man with sexual acts for money (see *Buyer*).

E

Escort
An organization, operating chiefly via cell phone and the internet, which sends a victim to a buyer's location or arranges for the buyer to come to a house or apartment; this may be the workplace of a single woman or a small brothel. Some escort services are networked with others and can assemble large numbers of women for parties and conventions.

F

Family
The term used to describe the other individuals under the control of the same pimp. He plays the role of father (or *Daddy*) while the group fulfills the need for a *family*.

Finesse (Romeo) Pimp

One who prides himself on controlling others primarily through psychological manipulation. Although he may shower his victims with sweet talk, affection, persuasion, and gifts (especially during the recruitment phase), the threat of violence is always present.

G

Grooming

The time in which a trafficker/pimp invests in a potential victim to gain trust and loyalty. The trafficker will build a false relationship using, gifts, affection, and feeding on the victim's dreams/vulnerabilities until the trafficker has formed an attachment with the victim that can be manipulated.

Gorilla (Guerilla) Pimp

A pimp who controls his victims almost entirely through physical violence and force.

I

Incall

An *incall* occurs when a buyer travels to the location the sex worker or victim is already working—like a brothel, apartment, or hotel room—and receives services there.

O

Out of Pocket

The phrase describing when a victim is not under control of a pimp but working on a pimp-controlled track, leaving her vulnerable to threats, harassment, and violence in order to make her "choose" a pimp. This may also refer to a victim who is disobeying the pimp's rules.

Outcall

An *outcall* means the buyer wants to have someone travel to them and service them at their home, office, or most commonly, hotel room.

P

Pimp Hand

The use of a backhanded slap as a violent method of control.

Pimp Hard

When a trafficker/pimp raises the quota for a victim, reduces their amount of rest, or places them in a more dangerous situation for business.

Pimps Up, Hoes Down

Pimps (traffickers) dominate and stay on top, keeping all of the respect and money, Hoes (victims) stay down, being completely submissive and working to make the money for the pimps.

Q

Quota

A set amount of money that a trafficking victim must make each night before she can come "home." If the victim returns without meeting the quota, she is typically beaten and sent back out on the street to earn the rest.

R

Reckless Eyeballing

A term which refers to the act of looking around instead of keeping your eyes on the ground. Eyeballing is against the rules and could lead an untrained victim to "choose up" by mistake.

Roses

Term for money meant to avoid self-incrimination with law enforcement when asking for money in exchange for sexual acts.

S

Snow Bunny

A white girl.

Square

A cigarette or a person who is not aware of "The Life."

Squaring Up

Attempting to escape or exit prostitution.

Stable
A group of victims who are under the control of a single pimp.

Stack
$1,000

Survivor
A person who overcomes human trafficking. The path of survivorship isn't perfect, and it's OK to mess up. The key is continuing to move toward healing.

T

The Game or **"The Life"**
The terms commonly used by those working in the commercial sex industry to refer to prostitution. The subculture of prostitution, complete with rules, a hierarchy of authority, and language. Referring to the act of pimping as *"The Game"* gives the illusion that it can be a fun and easy way to make money, when the reality is much harsher. Women and girls will say they've been *"in The Life"* if they've been involved in prostitution for a while.

Track
An area of town known for prostitution activity. This can be the area around a group of strip clubs and pornography stores, or a particular stretch of street.

Trafficker (Pimp)

A person who uses force, fraud, or coercion to exploit and make money off another person through labor, services, or commercial sex. A sex trafficker is a person who profits off of selling another person's body for sex.

Trauma-Bonding

A strong attachment that happens in a victim's brain when a perpetrator mixes love and affection with abuse. This is often seen in domestic violence or Stockholm Syndrome.

Trauma-Informed

Working with someone in a way that takes into account the trauma they've been through and how it may affect them and your interactions with them.

Turn Out

To be forced into prostitution (*verb*) or a person newly involved in prostitution (*noun*).

Turning a Trick

Performing a sex act in exchange for money or goods. A *trick* may also be used in reference to the person purchasing the sex act.

V

Victim

A person being forced, tricked, or manipulated into human trafficking. This person is not a criminal, and he or she deserves to be helped.

Sources

"Common Sex Trafficking Language." *Shared Hope International*
sharedhope.org/the-problem/trafficking-terms/.

Trafficking Terms. Lighthouse for Life
www.lighthouseforlife.org/images/resources/Trafficking-Terms.pdf.

Escort Section
Backpage.com

INTRODUCTION

2014

I found myself sitting in a jail cell, again, in Waco, Texas. Everything happened so fast. As I waited for whatever would come next, feelings of terror, sadness, anxiety, confusion, pain, depression, guilt, failure, shame, and fear of the unknown threatened to drown me. I know that sounds like a lot to feel at once. It was. I was not only in a physical jail, but I was also imprisoned in an emotional and mental cage with these overpowering feelings that I couldn't seem to get away from, no matter how far I ran. These feelings had controlled me for so long. As much as I hated feeling this way, it also felt normal. For a moment, I had felt something different, as the idea that maybe I could finally get out of "The Life" seemed a little more possible. But that dream felt distant as I waited, the feeling of cold steel against my wrist, handcuffed to a table in a bare interview room.

"What is going to happen to me? What is Jonathan going to do to me when we get out? Is my family safe?" These questions swirled in my head. It was hard to believe I would ever survive this, especially after what I had just told the police about him. *What had I been thinking?* I wanted to "square up" and had lost sight of what was most important in the moment: survival. I knew better than to be "out of pocket" and snitch on him. My inner demon, the voice in my head, his voice, kept reminding me: *"Keep your head down and stay silent. Lay low. He will always see and know."*

What had caused me to tell the detectives the truth? What had made me think they genuinely wanted to help me, or that they could protect me? Why had I risked Jonathan's revenge, risked being treated like a criminal, risked my life? For years, I'd lived with the abuse, the pain, the manipulation, the drugs, the rape. But today, something felt different. Here, in this cold jail cell, when I had seemingly hit rock bottom, I felt something new rising up from deep within me for a moment. I had been in jail plenty of times by this point, but instead of treating me like a criminal, the detectives here suggested that this might not all be my fault. This feeling was so foreign to me, but now I recognize it was hope. Was this hope worth risking my life for? I was afraid I had said too much already, but I wanted desperately to believe I could trust someone enough to help me and get me away from the pure hell I'd been living.

Here I was at a fork in the road. One path offered trust with a glimmer of hope and hint of freedom, but also the very real possibility of disappointment, danger, and retaliation. The darker path offered survival, at least for now; a world I knew how to manage, but with the assurance of a life I hated with no escape. Could this really be a way out, or was this another trap or system destined to fail me? Could there be a better life for me beyond this?

My mind buzzed with questions and painful memories of my past, and my heart raced with emotions. I heard the guard's boots as he approached my cell, and I knew it was time to make my choice.

SURVIVING "THE LIFE"

1

BROKEN

1992

My story begins in Ustavskoe, a small village in Yaroslavl, Russia. My birth name is Yulia, and I have seven siblings, one of whom is my twin brother. My twin brother and I were adopted as babies by an American family who gave us new names. They changed my name to Julia. I know very little about this time of my life. Growing up, I only knew the names of my birth parents. My whole life I imagined all sorts of things about them. I imagined that, desperately poor, it broke my mother's heart to let go of us. I imagined she thought we had a better chance at a good life without her, as she could barely get by feeding my older siblings. I imagined my father was killed in some brave and noble way when we were infants, and my mother didn't know how to get by without him. I imagined maybe she tried to do her best for us.

I often wondered what my parents and siblings were doing at any given moment. Were they in a warm, light-filled house, sitting at the dining room table laughing and talking over a home-cooked meal? Or were they cold, on the streets, starving, desperately fighting to find crumbs or a loaf of bread for dinner? I wondered both the good and the bad. I ached with the desire to see them, to know them, and to understand why they could not or chose not to keep us. Did they miss us? Did they cry over abandoning us? Or have they moved past any thought of the twin boy and girl they left at the orphanage? These questions lived in the back of my mind for as long as I can remember.

These thoughts swirled in my imagination until late one night, while working on this book, I received a message on Facebook from a stranger named Natasha. In the message, she told me she was my biological sister, and she had also been adopted by an American family when she was young. Since she lived with my birth mom for a few years, she was able to answer many of my questions. I found out more about my beginnings and familial situation. My birth mom struggled with many challenges. She started having children at just 19 years old and gave birth eight times between 1985 and 1994. Both of my birth parents were alcoholics, and they sold most of their possessions to feed their addiction.

My mother had a job as a milk woman for a short time but couldn't keep it because of her alcoholism and homelessness. My siblings and I all had different fathers, some decent, others angry. I am one of a pair of fraternal twins, the fourth pregnancy of my birth mother. From what I've learned, my mom kept my two older brothers, my older sister, and one of my younger sisters. When my brother and I were born in March 1992, she verbally refused us that same day, just as she did later with my two other younger sisters. We were taken from the maternity home to an orphanage. It took a long time for the state to successfully contact my parents again and acquire their signatures officially confirming abandonment of all parental rights. During this time, my brother and I were placed into a foster home while the state waited for these signatures. A year later, in 1993, they made contact, and our birth parents signed over their rights so we could be put up for adoption. No Russian couples wanted us, and we were placed back in the orphanage to await international adoption.

Throughout this time, my mother couch-surfed from one man's house to the next, dragging my siblings along with her. My sister remembers my mom telling her and another of my siblings to be quiet and to not wake her sleeping boyfriend, who had just wet the bed in his drunken state. Over time, the state declared her unfit as a mother and ordered her to change her behavior or lose her children. Our mother continued to drink, and eventually all of my other siblings were placed into orphanages.

Thanks to my sister, I know the truth about my early years. I have since visited my birth sister and met her family, and we keep in touch. It was wonderfully strange to meet my sister as an adult, to hear about her life, and to see our similar mannerisms and parallel struggles. It makes me feel more rooted in my identity, in who I am. The truth isn't nearly as romantic as my imagination, but it still feels good to finally know. My mom struggled, surrendered to those struggles, and lost us as a result. I wonder how much of her I inherited; if her struggles and pain run through my blood. That may help explain some of what I have been through. So now I know the truth.

After 20 months in the Russian state's care, my brother and I won the lottery. A couple from Texas wanted to adopt us. They were part of a Christian family and had tried for years to have biological children of their own. They found an adoption agency that placed orphaned Russian children. On November 11, 1993, we left for our new country, our new family, our new lives, and our new names. While

I don't have memories of arriving at the airport in the United States as a baby, I do have many pictures of a beautiful family who was so excited to have us, who welcomed us with open arms, joyful tears, and feelings of warmth and love that could have radiated for miles. In a moment, these two socially orphaned babies had two parents, loving grandparents, an aunt, an uncle, and cousins.

Newly arrived in America, my brother and I became United States citizens. We were forming totally new identities.

I'll never know what my life would have been like growing up with my birth family in Russia, but I know they could not have given me the opportunities that my adoptive parents and family offered me. Although I'll always remember I have biological parents in Russia, I consider my adoptive parents my mother and father, and I deeply appreciate all they did for us then and continue to do for us now. While we were growing up, our house was in the upper middle-class suburbs, away from areas of extreme poverty and danger. My brother and I were carefree, often playing outside with the other neighborhood kids. My dad helped my brother and me build a treehouse in the backyard, where I fondly remember many adventures. My family gave us wonderful toys and gifts. I was given the opportunity to learn music, play the piano, read, and play sports such as soccer, tennis, swimming, and volleyball. We were given everything an upper middle-class, American family can offer. I'm grateful. Bringing two kids from the other side of the world and calling them your own is a brave, generous thing to do. I know it is far from easy. My father was a senior manager with a large phone service company, while my mother was a budget administrator for a business. Mom retired early and stayed home with us. They were very active in their church—Dad directed all the vocal and bell choirs, and Mom sang in the choir and volunteered. We had everything children could want or need.

For me, ultimately, what this new life offered was not enough. I entered their home already broken. Babies thrive physically and mentally through nurturing, healthy pregnancies, and safe, loving homes. In my short life in Russia, I experienced fear, hunger, neglect, instability, trauma, identity changes, and a move to the other side of the world where a different language was spoken. As is the case with many international adoptions, it was a struggle for our orphanage to adequately care for all of the children and meet all of their developmental needs, both physical and emotional. Some orphanages operate like an assembly line. If a child is alive and breathing, it's time for workers to move on to the next child. Many children who started out in orphanages have medical problems that stem either from birth or as a direct result of the medical neglect and possible abuse endured in the orphanage where they were placed. Soon after arriving in America, I had a body cast on my hips and legs to correct a congenital hip dysplasia, a condition possibly made worse from living in the orphanage.

By adopting me, my parents also adopted the serious and damaging effects from the turbulence of my first two years of life. My parents are very loving and did the best they could, but they were not equipped to parent a child with what we now know to be complex trauma. They both had their own struggles. Instead of getting a whole and happy child, they got a physically and emotionally broken kid. It had been just the two of them for 15 years, plus their first child (the dog). Suddenly, they were parents to twin toddlers. In addition, five months after we arrived, my dad's company transferred him a thousand miles away from their support system, which was all of our other family. Unexpectedly, my dad's new job required a great deal of travel, so my mom was home alone with us in a new community.

Nothing could have prepared them for the next 16 years. Even as a toddler, I was really difficult. My little body and mind tried to survive in the same ways

I had in the orphanage, which didn't work so well in a secure home. I struggled to cope with the chaos and pain I had experienced. As I grew older, my behavior got worse. I resisted my parents' affection, I got angry, and I threw fits all the time, trying to deal with the intense waves of emotional pain and frustration I was experiencing. I traveled the expressive path of opposition and conflict. I wanted to be independent, not micro-managed or controlled.

I know people saw me as a troubled and rebellious kid, *choosing* to cause problems and drama in my family. But that's not true. I acted that way because of the pain I felt inside. I didn't *choose* to be born into a broken family. I didn't *choose*, as an infant, to be separated from my family and placed in a crowded orphanage. I didn't *choose* to be taken away from everything I'd known and brought into a totally foreign world. I was a survivor, and as a young child, I coped the only way my underdeveloped, damaged brain knew how. I didn't have the mental and emotional ability to *choose* how I survived the aftermath of the trauma and pain of my life, or even to understand what I had been through. I behaved with a normal response to the not-normal events that happened to me at such a young age. I wish others could have understood and seen it that way.

By the time I was five years old, my parents got me into counseling, which was a good idea. They were insistent I was not behaving as a child my age should. They were sure something was wrong with me. I could tell they were disappointed, frustrated and sad when dealing with me. Everything was my fault. Unfortunately, my parents were not given the right tools to understand complex trauma and how it presents itself in children. Instead of doctors and counselors recognizing I was suffering with "Complex Post Traumatic Stress Disorder (C-PTSD)," many of them assumed I was a rebellious, strong-willed, and willfully defiant child. What I needed was an advocate who understood how to help me, but I had none, so I felt betrayed and alone.

The first counselor I went to for several years was a nightmare, at least in my five-year-old mind. She made me feel worse than I had before. She took my parents' side, accusing me of lying or putting on a show just to make life difficult. I never trusted my parents enough to tell them the demeaning things she would say to me. Her words hurt me and solidified the pain and rejection I was feeling. How could I attach myself to adults like counselors or my parents who seemed to resent my existence?

Over the next years, while there were tumultuous times, there were also good times. Our family would spend many nights playing games and enjoying the outdoors. We would play kickball in the front yard, four-square tennis in the driveway, swim in the pool, and play the game "push dad off the big step." We took family vacations to sites around the United States. At seven years old, I went to tennis camp, where the instructor sought out my mom and told her I had a real talent. My parents encouraged me to continue and supported me in my tennis practice. I took art lessons, gymnastics, and dance lessons, and swam on the Bedford SURF summer swim team. I went to the best schools my parents could afford. One year, my mom felt like spending more time with me would be better for me, so I was homeschooled. I rang chimes and hand bells at our church where my dad directed music.

While these were all wonderful things, I still suffered. I was anxious and depressed. Things just got worse. There were fun times in our family, but the conflict and turmoil began to outweigh the good times. As things progressively worsened, one event triggered a rapid downward spiral. I was 14 when I had my first experience with sexual abuse. I met this guy through church, and we started dating, although I was barely allowed to do anything with him. My parents and I had fought earlier in the day, and I was upset, desperate to get away from it all.

My boyfriend used his dad's car to pick me up, and I snuck out of the house in the middle of the night. After driving around, he parked in a church parking lot where he then molested me and tried to rape me. Terrified of being blamed or not believed, I told no one at first. I felt like I'd caused enough trouble. I was confused about what had happened, and I had some trust issues. Finally, I found the courage to tell my mom and one other person. I was scared, confused and embarrassed, so I was very vague in nervously recounting the molestation. I didn't even mention the attempted rape. My mom believed me, but the other person I shared this with responded with questions like: "Are you sure you didn't somehow encourage this? Did you want it at first and then became scared and backed out, changing your mind? Did you send an unclear message to him that you were interested? Could you be misunderstanding or exaggerating this?" As I feared, this person's reaction confirmed that people wouldn't see me as the victim.

Someone talked to the boy's parents, but because I wouldn't talk about it in detail, no one knew it was serious enough to call the police. I continued to spiral into depression. Feeling guilty, dirty, ashamed, and alone, I had no one to talk to. I needed friends, but I had no idea how to have a healthy relationship with anyone or how to genuinely trust someone. After all, who would want to be friends with a kid who was always in trouble?

I tried to pretend I was fine on the outside, but the pain kept growing inside. I was 14, and coping with the pain seemed impossible, so I began self-harming. I would often cut myself in order to focus on physical pain instead of the emotional pain that I felt. My world was rapidly spiraling out of control, my grasp on hope quickly loosening. I was severely depressed. I didn't know who to turn to or who I could trust. I went to school, did my homework, went to church. I survived.

At 15, I ended up making one friend at school. He also had a difficult family situation, and he was numbing his pain with drugs, alcohol, and cigarettes. He had prescription pain pills, and a little of everything else, even hardcore hallucinogenic drugs. We would hang out whenever we were able to get away from our parents for a while without them noticing. We skipped classes and lied to our parents about after-school extracurricular activities. He offered to share his drugs with me, so we began using together. While I had been introduced to cigarettes and alcohol before this, through kids at my private school or the apartment complex in the neighborhood, this was my first time to use drugs. I began to smoke weed, pop pills, and drink. I had been around kids who were using drugs before this, but this was the first time I began using drugs myself. I didn't develop an addiction, but it did seem to help with my pain for a while. It felt really good to finally have a friend who understood, and it felt good to finally find a way to forget the pain I was in, even if just for a few hours. He eventually moved away, leaving me alone again. I felt like I would always be disconnected and isolated from the world, continually reliving the painful experiences of my life. Almost on a daily basis, I considered suicide and continued to cut myself. When I was 15, I was admitted to a hospital for suicide watch. I had been prescribed medication for my depression and anxiety, but I refused to take it because I was embarrassed. I thought my parents were trying to control me.

My whole life, I'd felt I was a bad kid, never good enough, always rocking the boat for those around me. But now, my boat was sinking. I was spiraling into a dark pit of anguish and mistrust I couldn't escape. I felt isolated from everyone: friends, family, and most especially, myself.

At 15 years old, in desperation, my parents took me out-of-state to a specialist whom they had researched at length, who had experience working with children with similar problems. This specialist recommended treatment in the form of a boot camp. It focused on exerting complete control over me, allowing me little privacy and no unearned privileges, and achieving a high level of compliance. I was not allowed any freedom. Although my parents were trying to help me out of love and sought out the best methods money could buy at the time, this was one of the most traumatic times in my childhood. Home life continued to be a living hell for all of us.

I became more and more miserable while numbly sitting in school and church. This cycle continued through my teen years. I went through the motions and tried to follow the rules, but nothing changed. My parents tried different strategies, tried to heal their strong-willed child and our wounded family, but I resisted. For years, we were a family in crisis. We all struggled to survive.

At 16, I tried to run away from home. Law enforcement picked me up and took me back home. They didn't try to figure out what was going on. They simply told me that by law I had to do what my parents said and that I should be ashamed of my behavior. The weight of guilt, shame, and embarrassment grew.

The issues between my parents and me worsened. It felt like a bomb could go off any minute in our home. We didn't know how to communicate. Every day, we trusted each other less and resented each other more. I know it was hard for my parents. I know I hurt them. And it was hard for me. Every time I was blamed for the problems in our lives, every time I was cut off from my peers, every time I was threatened to be sent away, every time I had more restrictions piled on me, it sent me deeper and deeper into despair and isolation. One psychologist told my parents to give up on me. In spite of the turmoil going on at home, I was able to mask it well enough that people on the outside were completely unaware. I wanted someone to notice so badly, but I was too embarrassed and afraid to let it show. I tried to keep my head down and survive.

Somehow, I pushed through the pain and made it to high school graduation in 2010. Here was my chance for a fresh start. All I wanted was to leave behind the negativity, toxic relationships with my family, emotional pain, and loneliness, and finally start a new life. My parents controlled and micromanaged 18 years of my life in their efforts to save and change me, but it was finally time to find my own happiness.

Going to college offered me that chance. I didn't care about furthering my education, but I was desperate to feel happy, free, and in control of my own destiny. To be honest, I don't think that any of us expected that my moving away would be a success. But at age 18, I entered a four-year college that was hours away from home, with a broken brain, broken heart, and broken spirit. In my brokenness, I was set up to be "groomed" for "The Life."

2

BETRAYED

During my first semester of college, I let my guard down and made a new friend. I probably should have seen that she was trouble, but she was the only person I had. We hung out every day and ate meals together as much as possible. Even though I had a little experience with drugs from high school, I still was a "square" and pretty sheltered from the things she was involved in. The thought of stripping or exotic dancing had never crossed my mind, but she wanted to take me to the club and show me how to make money. I agreed to go and check it out. I went a few times to party with her, but I never considered dancing for money. She never went on stage to dance when I was with her, so I didn't suspect she might be working there. We drank, and she would talk to different guys and introduce me to them. A few of them suggested we should go up there and dance, but I refused. I enjoyed going there to party, but the thought of dancing for money seemed totally off limits to me.

One night, we were drinking with some other people from my dorm, and they dared us to kiss each other and said they'd pay us to do more. I refused. I'd never made money like this before, and I didn't want to start. She forced me to, assaulting me in front of a group of guys. Humiliated, I didn't tell anyone. I didn't understand why my friend would betray me like this. I knew this wasn't the type of friendship I wanted, and I stopped talking to her. Alone again, I quickly fell back into the darkness of my depression and self-harming. My grades dropped, I skipped class, and I drowned in isolation.

After what happened with that girl, I avoided friendships with females altogether. Various guys would befriend me, but their intentions were never good. I lived in an on-campus apartment dorm and my roommates made fun of me and bullied me to try to get me to move out. They didn't think I was cool enough to hang with their crowd. To them, I was boring. I didn't like to party through all hours of the night, and I didn't like to socialize for long periods of time. I was quiet and liked to stay to myself. The bullying continued and worsened every day. They used my things without asking and got mad if I asked them not to. They were constantly spreading gossip and stories about me across the campus. One of my roommates called the campus police and told them I was selling weed out of the apartment. The police came, searched my belongings, and questioned me. They couldn't find anything, so they left. The whole dorm complex saw this happening, and I was humiliated. I kept to myself the rest of my time in the dorm. I didn't talk to anyone, and no one paid attention to me. It was as if my very existence had been blotted off the map.

My parents were paying my tuition and my room and board, but besides that, we barely talked. Anytime we did, it ended in a fight. After one fight, I told my mom to never call me again.

Then, one day, things turned around for me. I met Ryan in my freshman English class. He started paying attention to me and flirting with me. I thought he was cute, and after we started dating, we were inseparable. I finally found the connection I so desperately wanted.

I loved it when he would tell me how beautiful I was. He said exactly what my heart longed to hear: "I love our time together. I just can't seem to get enough of you. You're really cool and laid back, easy to talk to and fun to hang out with." Finally, I found someone to make me feel understood, seen, loved, and normal. Growing up, I was told many times that I have problems, and that I'll never be normal.

I felt judged and labeled and those labels haunted me: damaged, psychotic, unlovable, problem child, baggage, lazy, weird, adopted, troublemaker, failure, stupid, liar, manipulative, fat, sick, attention-seeker. After all that, you can probably understand why it felt so good to be accepted by Ryan, just as I was. Instead of judging and labeling me, Ryan related to me on so many levels. He shared with me the different hardships he had suffered throughout his childhood, making me feel as if we had a special, strong connection no one else could understand. He chose to be my partner in many of our class assignments and asked for help editing papers. He made me feel smart and important. As time passed, he opened up to me more and more. He shared his struggles. He asked for my advice. He gave me a sense of belonging, purpose, and trust that I had never experienced before. Instead of questioning or blaming me when I shared my past with him, Ryan believed and encouraged me. He said, "I love you. You are a blessing in my life. I don't know what I would do without you. You always seem to see the good in people like me." His words were intoxicating.

Ryan became my boyfriend, and I spent many nights in his dorm room. He would walk with me around campus, holding my hand and asking me about my life. When my classes let out, he would be there waiting for me and walk me to my next class. If I had a problem on campus, he would be there ready to help me in whatever way I needed. He started paying for my food, buying me gifts, and introducing me to his circle of friends. Finally, I didn't feel alone. This was my dream come true! His family would consistently send him money, and in turn, Ryan would share some of it with me. If I needed something, he would be there for me, providing for my needs and making sure I was OK. Eventually, he told me he had been telling his family about me and sharing with them how important I was. He told me, "My dad and family love hearing about you. They are really hoping to meet you. They know I love you, and so they care about and support you, too." How could I ask for anything better?

Sadly, it wasn't long until things drastically changed. Ryan experienced a hard childhood and had a lot of struggles growing up as well. There was high stress and conflict within his family. While we were in school together, the toxic stress in his family became worse and Ryan found it harder to manage. He began finding ways to numb his feelings of frustration and pain. We all need outlets for our pain. I was Ryan's. He became deliberately abusive and manipulative, finding some sense of control in his life by controlling me. Ryan was more experienced with drugs than me, as I hadn't used since high school. He started using drugs around me and persuaded me to start using as well. I loved him and depended on him, so how could I refuse? Ryan fell into a heavy drug addiction and over a few weeks, his once sweet behavior totally changed. He was flunking out of school and running out of money. We both were. He took my money and made me pawn my stuff. He started threatening and abusing me if I did something he didn't like. I already didn't talk to my family, but he made sure I was cut off from any other friends I had started to make as well. I didn't like what our relationship had become. I didn't want to be controlled. But at the same time, it felt normal in a way. I had experienced control my whole life. At least this time, he wanted me.

One night, I reacted badly to a drug I was using with Ryan and started seizing. Ryan called 911 because I was so out of it and could barely walk. The EMS Team took me to the hospital. When the hospital staff checked me out, they accused me of faking it, just seeking attention. To them, I was just another messed up, partying college student. This blame and accusation felt all too familiar. I wanted to get away from the judgment and belittlement, out of the hospital and as far away as possible from authority figures. Ryan helped me slip away unnoticed from the ER. After this, Ryan started treating me more abusively in public, confident he could get away with it. Everyone in the school knew I had been in the hospital for drugs, and I became "that girl." Any shred of a reputation I had was now gone. So why try? From there, we started using hard drugs and ended up moving in with our drug-dealing friends. They were my only friends, and as messed up as they were, they supported me when Ryan got out of control. We stopped going to class and started using constantly. We both were flunking out, didn't have any money left, and saw no reason to stick around there.

Ryan's parents had always coddled him, and his dad convinced him to move back home to help him get back on track. He decided to return to San Antonio. At that point, I was convinced he was all I had. I didn't have a relationship with my family. I didn't have a chance of passing my classes. I didn't have any friends who cared about me enough to notice what was going on. And although he treated me like I was worthless, I still thought that being with him was better than being alone.

He told me his dad wouldn't mind if I came and stayed with them. So, when Ryan decided to move back home to San Antonio, I went with him. This was a move that would prove to be the beginning of a chapter in my life best described as a nightmare.

As soon as we pulled up to Ryan's house, it was clear his dad wasn't expecting me. He wouldn't even let me in the house. Ryan tried to sneak me in a few times, but when that didn't work, he found another solution. He kept me in the trunk of his car at night and made me shower in his front yard with the garden hose. This went on for weeks. He became more violent, beating, threatening, and completely controlling me. He treated me like a caged animal, and I started to feel like one. He would take all my money and threaten to dump me on the side of the road somewhere if I didn't do exactly what he wanted, when he wanted, how he wanted. It was chaos. I was terrified, disoriented, and high most of the time. I didn't want to be left on the streets of a strange city alone. He beat me, raped me, dragged me by my hair, spit in my face, screamed at me that I was only good for sex, drugs, and money. When I did try running away, he found me and beat me. When his dad found me in the trunk, Ryan convinced him I wanted to be there and that he couldn't get rid of me.

At some level, Ryan was right. I thought I needed him to survive. And after all, isn't this what I deserved? I felt like I was always causing pain and problems for the people I ended up having to depend on. At least I knew how to survive if I stayed with him. He steadily introduced me to more and harder drugs. Before long,

I was hooked on cocaine, completely dependent and using all day. He would dump me on the streets, come back for me, and dump me again. I was trash to him. I felt like trash to myself. I was terrified of being abandoned but terrified of him also. He began taking me to different locations, abandoning me to be abused under bridges and behind dumpsters. The well-dressed, private school girl from the suburbs was transformed into the dirty woman on the side of the road—high, homeless, doing whatever it takes to survive.

One night, I was arrested with a group of his friends for possession of marijuana. In a rush of courage, I tried to tell the officers I was not there of my own free will. They mocked me and said I was just trying to get off the hook. Worse, they told Ryan what I had said about him beating and abusing me. This put me in even more danger than I had been in before. The police officers didn't believe me and did nothing to help, and Ryan was furious. After all, I had snitched on him. And that was never a safe choice. I had broken the unspoken cardinal rule. Never cross him. Never tell anyone. Never dare to seek help. He made sure I regretted it.

Seeing the state we were in, Ryan's parents finally contacted my parents. My parents came down to San Antonio twice to attempt to intervene. They showed up unannounced, trying to force me to go with them. I know they cared about me and were desperate to get me out of there. They knew by that point that I wouldn't go willingly. I was completely lost. They tried to take me home, even hiring a mediator and using force, but I resisted. I didn't want to leave Ryan's control and be back in theirs.

I had never been surer in my life that I didn't trust my parents, and I wanted nothing to do with them. Both situations were controlling, but Ryan had two things to offer me that my parents couldn't: a form of twisted romantic love and drugs to numb my pain. After that, I seldom spoke to my parents other than an occasional check-in.

3

TRAFFICKED

Life grew darker and darker. He couldn't keep me in his car forever, so Ryan paid someone to keep me in an abandoned apartment, with no electricity or water. Men would come in and out day after day for sex with me, while I was barely conscious, drugs constantly pumped into my body. I saw Ryan giving and taking money from some of them, but I didn't really care what happened. I was hopeless and numb. One night, a guy we did drugs with helped me get away and let me move in with him. I don't think I would have survived there much longer.

This guy's name was Derrick. Derrick acted like my "knight in shining armor" at first. He housed me, fed me, and let me recover a little. However, it soon became clear he had other motives. He had no money and had a major issue with alcohol and drugs. Over time, he started expecting me to earn my keep by taking care of him—cooking, cleaning, and paying the bills. It didn't matter if I was too tired or sick. If Derrick was going to let me stay there, then I had to do these things when and how he wanted me to. He progressively became colder and more demanding. I wasn't the first woman he did this to. The stories of his relationships with his baby mamas, neighbors, and others reflected mine. He would manipulate whomever whenever to get whatever he wanted. After a while, he demanded even more of me. He didn't pretend to want romance with me, but he did require me to have sex with him. Since I had been forced to trade sex for survival many times with Ryan, I thought it was just what I had to do. I didn't love him, but I did have to sleep with him if I wanted to stay there. And I didn't have anywhere else to go.

Derrick was on all kinds of drugs all the time, so he was totally unpredictable. He had partial custody of his kids, and sometimes they came to stay with us. I took care of everyone—him, the kids—and tried to keep myself alive. He made me get a few random jobs and give him whatever I earned. I started working at Whataburger. Attempting to stay away from Derrick as long as possible, I worked as many hours as the Whataburger would give me. Every day, I forced myself to show up at work with a smile and good attitude, hiding my bruises. Derrick showed up at some point during most of my shifts, threatening me or my coworkers. He often showed up drunk and high and would attack me in a jealous outburst. As he got more violent, I couldn't hide the black eyes and other injuries. It got really tough working in this state, so I also started showing up high, sneaking drugs during breaks, numbing the pain and giving me energy to get through a shift. While at work, I was often in a dream-like state, and people noticed. I overheard my coworkers whispering about me, wondering what was going on and where my injuries came from. They didn't want to get involved though, so no one reached out. The manager was always kind to me and would give me rides to and from work if I needed. She knew I was in a bad situation and tried to help me out the best she knew how. After an especially bad episode with Derrick, I would call her quickly from the bathroom, whispering that I couldn't make it to work. I was so relieved and grateful that she didn't fire me. After long hours at Whataburger, I came home to take care of his kids. In return, Derrick took everything from me—my money, my phone, my independence. He threatened and beat me. He kept me isolated, only allowing me to go to work. I was stilled trapped in San Antonio, just with a different man. Control, isolation, and abuse seemed to follow me wherever I went.

Our living situation made life even more miserable. I had to sleep on a pullout bed infested with cockroaches and mice. I often woke up in the night with a cockroach crawling over my face or burrowing in my hair. I remember picking cockroaches out of my food and finding holes in my clothes from the mice. As bad as it was inside, the real danger was outside the apartment. The whole complex was gang-run, and it wasn't uncommon to witness fights or hear gunshots. I remember one night when the neighbor across the hall become angry with her boyfriend. She cut off her own thumb and stabbed him in the arm. The woman and her children ran to me, seeking safety.

One day, Derrick sent me to a trailer park where Ryan and I had lived for a short while to get drugs for him. The surrounding neighborhood looked like a war zone because the gangs were constantly bombing each other, leaving houses blown into pieces with missing rooftops and walls and a landfill of scattered furniture and belongings. It was a devastating landscape of violence and destruction. The cops barely patrolled the area because it was so bad. When I got there, the dealers from a local gang that owned the trailer park kidnapped and raped me. They took me to a nice neighborhood, to a park with a port-a-potty. They trafficked me there all day, with 50 to 60 men, some even high-school boys, coming in and out. They dropped me back off and as always, I was silent. That's how you survive in that world—you *keep your mouth shut.* I don't know if Derrick knew that was going to happen, but he never should have sent me there.

One night, Derrick beat me so badly I thought I was going to die. I called my mom to tell her I loved her. Then I called 911. High and not wanting to get caught, Derrick turned on the burners to try to burn down the apartment. He then jumped out of a three-story window and escaped, going into hiding. The police had no leads, and they agreed to drop me at the apartment of a friend from work. My mom convinced me to let her come down and get me. I was so desperate and scared Derrick would find and kill me, that I went back to North Texas with her. My parents co-signed on an apartment lease for me, with the condition that I would give them a set of keys so they could check up on me whenever they wanted. I agreed and moved to the town next to them to try to get a fresh start. I transferred to the local Whataburger and worked hard.

I tried to move on, but I was plagued with the stress of readjusting to life and having flashbacks of everything that happened. I was still battling feelings of hopelessness. Did I even belong in this world? To deal with all the change, flashbacks, and depression, I started using again.

As I started to get adjusted, a friend suggested I start dating again. She said I just had a "round of bad apples." She helped me create an online dating profile. That's how many people meet each other these days, so I figured it was worth a try. However, online dating takes a lot of judgment. You have to be really careful who you are talking to, and even then, anyone can hide behind the facade of the internet. After what I'd been through the last two years, I had little to no judgment left. I didn't know how to spot the things that should have raised red flags or determine what was normal or not. I just wanted to be free, safe, and loved. Traffickers (pimps) know how to spot that kind of vulnerability. They see the fear, the weak spots, the little girl inside that feels so scared and alone that she will do whatever she's told.

I met my first online date in the parking lot of a Bone Daddy's restaurant. He convinced me to get in the car with him. To this day, I consider this to be the biggest mistake of my life. My online date kidnapped me as soon as I got in the car. Charles turned out to be a gorilla pimp. There are several different types of pimps. The Romeo or finesse pimp will use the boyfriending tactic, showering his victim with gifts, sweet words, promises of riches and a future together, until he can manipulate her to start making money for him. A gorilla pimp skips all that and goes straight to abuse and threats to exert his control. Charles took me straight to a hotel and raped me. Afterward, he looked down at me, laying on the bed with a broken heart, mind, body, and spirit. He said through his teeth, "You know you're mine now, right?" He took me, along with another woman and girl, to a bar downtown. I was drugged and repeatedly raped throughout that first night.

The next day after I was turned out, he took me back to my car but had another girl go with me to keep an eye on me. I couldn't be alone. I was under his control, and I couldn't see a way out.

During my shifts at Whataburger, I'd glance out the window and see Charles driving past multiple times throughout the day to make sure I was there, to make sure I knew he was watching. Although I never learned this girl's full story, I suspect she was an underage runaway that Charles took in. She called Charles "Daddy," and it was clear he had groomed and brainwashed her. He controlled her completely, manipulating her to only care about his needs and desires. Maintaining my job at Whataburger was even harder this time. I wanted to yell for help, but I was scared and ashamed. I didn't realize that I was a victim. I thought I had just made some bad choices that got me in bad situations. I was embarrassed to ask for help getting out of this mess I got myself into.

Plus, what if Charles found out? Would he make good on his threats to kill me or my family? At work, I took 10-minute naps in the bathroom whenever I could. I felt split between these two worlds I was balancing between: Who could I trust? Would someone from the safe, normal world know how to get me out of the dangerous street world? When people asked what I did on the weekends, I made up answers about partying with friends. I kept my cards close, giving general or scripted answers. My main focus was survival.

Charles allowed me to keep my job at Whataburger for a while, letting me feel like I was maintaining some normalcy, but I still couldn't get help. Charles threatened to kill me. He took my driver's license and all identification, learning my parents' address and other personal information he could use to manipulate me. He knew where I lived. He knew where my family lived. I was terrified of him and believed he'd carry out his threats if I stepped out of line, so I didn't see a way out to escape his grip on my freedom and life.

Charles became my trafficker, selling me to random men, sometimes up to 15 per night. This wasn't my first time being sold for sex, but this was different from how it happened with Ryan or Derrick. This time, it wasn't just to survive or get drugs. Charles expected me to make him stacks. Eventually, he was demanding too much of me, and I couldn't keep showing up for work at Whataburger. It was already difficult to keep up with the quota of money he required of me, but when he would pimp hard, it was nearly impossible to make my quota and still maintain my regular job. One day, I didn't show up for my shift, and they never heard from me again.

Charles took me and the other girls in his stable to the same bar night after night and week after week. He kept me drugged the whole time, so many of the details are a blur. He sat on one end of the bar with my phone and ID, watching and listening. His bottom was one of the bartenders and would be working alone on the nights Charles brought us there. She would work at the bar and make deals with the tricks, also known as dates, about who could see me and what the cost was, and she collected the money. This was "The Life," and this was *my life*. We used drugs, we did what was asked of us, and we survived.

Some people insist that girls "working" in the bars enjoy their work and want to be there, as opposed to them being victims who are being enslaved. They believe these girls are choosing to sleep with strange men of their own free will. However, I can tell you from firsthand experience that no victim of trafficking *wants* to be prostituted to strange men at a bar. No one *enjoys* those long hours of abuse and rape. When tricks asked me if I liked my work, I said yes. I smiled big and told them I loved my job and would choose this over a regular job any day. Did I mean that? *Absolutely not.* I told them these things while under the direct threat of my trafficker, who was listening to my every word and watching my every move. If my trafficker witnessed anything other than eagerness and smiles, he'd fear I was ratting him out or trying to run away, and I would pay the consequences. Tricks want to hear that you're happy in your job. Somehow, it eases their consciences as they choose to exploit women. Some people also insist that you aren't a victim of trafficking if you are getting paid. This simply isn't true. Yes, many times the trick will hand the money to whoever serviced him, but it doesn't stay in her possession long. A trafficker's number one priority is to "break a bitch." So the money that the trick gives the victim always goes straight to the trafficker after the trick is gone. Other times, the trick will directly pay the trafficker, in which case, the money doesn't even pass through the victim's hands. Of course, if you're a victim, you can't tell a trick this. You just keep smiling and "dating" so that tricks pay up, and ultimately, the traffickers stay happy. "Happy" victims lead to happy tricks, which leads to happy, rich traffickers. If you ask a trafficking victim if they want to be there or are forced into the lifestyle, 99.9

percent of the time she (or he) will tell you it's her choice. Off my soapbox, and back to the story.

One night, a trick approached me and asked me this same question. "Do you like your job? Do you want to keep working here?" I forced my smile and assured him I did. He saw through my act and could tell I was there against my will. He knew my trafficker, and he said he wanted to help me escape. Every time he would "date" me, he paid my trafficker for my services but gave me some money to stash away for myself. Each time, he told me part of an escape plan. I felt like part of a Lifetime movie as he orchestrated my elaborate jailbreak from Charles's clutch. One night, Charles found the extra money stashed in my car. Panicking, I called the trick, and he quickly finalized the escape plans. He took me by my apartment to grab a backpack full of clothes and a few pictures of my family, then dropped me off at a bus station. I took the bus back to San Antonio, the only other place I had connections, to stay with a friend I'd made through a former job. My parents were on their way home from vacation, and we planned to get together to celebrate Mother's Day, as we were still working to forge some type of relationship. But without telling them, I disappeared. I felt very sad and guilty about that, but only two things really mattered: the safety of my family and finally being out of Charles's control.

4

SURRENDERED

For a while, Charles tried to find me and sent me threatening messages, "Where you at? You're mine. I'll find you. You can't hide forever." Soon after moving in with my friend in San Antonio, she told me she was getting evicted from her apartment, as she was really behind on the bills. I also then discovered I was pregnant. Although I'd been forced to sleep with many men, I knew immediately that Charles was the father because I had not had unprotected sex with anyone else at the time I conceived. When Charles raped me, he never used protection, and my estimated date of conception lined up precisely with the week he raped me. I told my friend I was pregnant but made her believe I had wanted to sleep with Charles. She tried to convince me to get an abortion, but I wouldn't do it. I believed that even though it wasn't planned and came through an evil act, this little life had value.

While I was being trafficked by Charles, I tried to let my family in, but I often felt rejected. They said that I had put the family through too much already and that knowing about what I'd been through and was going through would be too painful for some of them. After months of desperately trying to muster the courage, I told my family about my pregnancy. Although I didn't tell my family the whole truth of how I'd gotten pregnant, they made it clear they wouldn't support me being a mother. My mom said they would have nothing to do with my daughter, and they couldn't help me unless I was planning on placing her for adoption. She insisted I find an adoption program where I could live until I had the baby and then give her up for adoption, which I did not want to do. My mom questioned how she could be in my daughter's life if she and I didn't even have a relationship. My family was concerned that if they were to be involved in my daughter's life, they may end up with another child to raise on their own. They thought I might abandon my daughter and leave them to make a choice between Child Protective Services or raising her on their own. I understand their concerns, but they made me feel like I was in an impossible situation yet again. No family support, no money, no job, no place to live. Pregnant with my trafficker's baby.

My friend met a guy online as well, and after he proposed, she moved to another state to be with him. They invited me to come live with them, and since I couldn't stay in the apartment any longer, I made plans to join them.

I found a cheap bus ticket for the next week. By that point, I was really familiar with the bus system, but this was a different side of town. I was disoriented. I spent the last of my money on the bus ticket, so I had not had a decent meal in days. I stayed in my friend's abandoned apartment as long as I could, but all the utilities had run out, and it was hot. It was in the high 90s, and I was very pregnant. Trying to run a few errands before I left, I found myself stranded at a bus stop, just trying to survive the day. I was the picture of desperation.

A guy drove by in his fancy maroon Lincoln with shiny rims, honked, and offered me a ride. He could tell I was alone and desperate. I turned him down at first, but he persuaded me. What else was I going to do? I was pregnant with no money or food. He looked a lot like every other guy I hung around. Criminal behavior, drug dealing, and illegal activity surrounded me. I knew many drug dealers who were cool, chill people, who would never consider selling a human being. Maybe he'd be OK too? Plus, I was out of options, and I needed to survive for my unborn child.

He took me where I needed to go and bought me food, then dropped me back at the apartment. He told me his name was Jonathan and asked me if I would call him so we could hang out again. He helped me out, and I told him I'd call him later. I had no intentions of ever making that call.

Remember Derrick, my second trafficker who almost burned down the apartment? That same week, he heard I was back in town. He tracked down my location and forcefully moved himself into the empty apartment with me. We had no furniture, food, water, or electricity. It would get so hot in the apartment that the only way to cool down was to lay on the bathroom floor. I remember waking up one day to a maggot crawling across the carpet towards me. It was hard living in a dirty and abandoned apartment while trying to stay safe with Derrick there. I couldn't get him to leave, and I didn't want to put my unborn child at risk by making him mad. Not knowing what to do, I called Jonathan. He offered to put me up in a hotel for a while.

The first night at the hotel, it became clear that Jonathan expected me to have sex with him. I was too physically weak and emotionally exhausted to argue. Plus, I felt like I owed him something for the help, and I was afraid to go back where Derrick was. I gave Jonathan what he wanted and then he left. I breathed a sigh of relief. I had done what it took to survive and stay safe with my child inside me, even if just for a moment.

The next morning, Jonathan came back and asked me to run some errands with him. We picked up one of his friends. Then, suddenly, he and his friend took my phone, ID, bus ticket, and money. They forced me to go with them to Corpus Christi, and I was back in "The Life."

Over the next few years, he trafficked me and other women all over Texas and around the country. Even after what I'd experienced with Charles, being trafficked by Jonathan was a new and shocking experience. Charles had forced me, drugged, into rooms with strange men. Jonathan trained me to work for him. He played up my Russian heritage, calling me by my high-school nickname, "Yuli." He advertised me as his "White Russian." He set up dates for me, starting out with a softer approach. My first date could tell I was clearly new, and he just talked to me and didn't make me do anything. My second date told me what to do, and I just had to do it. After a while, it was my job to make them feel comfortable, to increase my efforts to make more roses. Jonathan charged anywhere from $200 to $500 per hour for our time, based on who the clientele was. If we were near an oil field, we would typically have to charge more. At times, I remember dates asking for someone else because I looked too much like their daughter or sister. I got better at making money, and Jonathan saw how profitable his "Russian Beauty" was. Over time, the trafficking increased in intensity and frequency.

At times, we walked the strip, or the track, but mostly we used the "Escort" section of Backpage. com to advertise. We would travel different circuits, from city to city within a day's time. Jonathan sold us in Austin, San Marcos, Houston, San Antonio, Dallas, Fort Worth, Corpus Christi, Abilene, Lubbock, Killeen, Odessa, Tyler—the list goes on. We traveled across the country to Florida, Louisiana, Alabama, Tennessee, and more. We were always traveling. We traveled so much it was hard to keep straight where we were, and where all we had been. Days and weeks started blending together. Traffickers stay on the move. It makes it harder to get caught, maximizes the amount of money that can be made in different places, and keeps victims from building other relationships or reaching out for help. From what I can piece together, Jonathan trafficked me across 20 states and 131 Texas cities over the course of two years.

I was pregnant during the first year, but I didn't get any regular medical attention. I was forced to make at least $1,000 per night, working 72 hours straight with little food and no sleep. I was forced to have sex with 15 to 20 men per night. I was 20 years old.

Jonathan constantly told me I needed to get his name tattooed on my body. At first, I was completely against it. However, he constantly belittled me and verbally attacked me for refusing. He would tell me he loved me and wanted the world to know I was his. He would tell other traffickers and women that I wasn't loyal and couldn't be trusted because of my refusal to have his name tattooed on me. I was manipulated and intimidated and afraid. Jonathan had used his pimp hand before, and I didn't want to experience that again. After hours of drinking one night at DiamondJacks Casino in Louisiana, I caved and agreed. I finally surrendered to Jonathan and to "The Life," believing my whole life, however long I had left, would be like this.

After I was branded with his name, Jonathan immediately started showing me off to the other pimps at the casino, saying what a valuable "Russian trophy" he had. He showed me and my brand off to everyone. He ordered me to get him another drink and food. As I was leaving, he bragged to the other pimps saying, "See how obedient my 'Snow Bunny' is? She immediately jumps and does what I tell her without one word. That's my White Russian." I had gained his approval and was safe for a while longer.

Although I hated how he treated me, I also wanted to gain his trust and work my way up. If this was going to be my life, I might as well surrender to it and get what I could out of it. More of his trust meant more freedom and less violence for me.

One day, we drove up to Waco, and he told me to post an ad on Backpage, as usual. He left me at the motel to work, telling me I'd better have money for him when he returned. I worked on automatic, thinking only of obedience and survival. Later that night, he came back with a dangerous grin on his face and told me to get dressed and come with him to the parking lot. There, we met up with a man with three young white girls. My trafficker bragged, talked, and finessed everyone in the room. One of the girls openly said she wanted to go with us. The other pimp wasn't happy. When the girl came with us, my heart broke. She told us she was 18, but I could tell she was younger. Years later, when I was out of the life, I found out she had run away from a local youth residential center with another girl.

My maternal instincts kicked in, and I started trying to figure out how to save her. When we were alone, I tried to convince her this was not what she wanted, but she argued with me, thinking Jonathan would take care of her. She told Jonathan what I said to her, and he threatened me, my unborn child, and my freedom. I tried to talk him into letting her leave, telling him a young runaway would cause him problems. He wouldn't listen. I tried to get her to call her family, but she wouldn't. She said both parents were crack addicts who beat her every day. She didn't want to go home. Money had to be made, and she wouldn't leave. So I set up tricks for us, giving her the repeats or regulars, who I knew would be somewhat safer.

I finally convinced Jonathan he needed to send the girl home to keep us out of trouble. As soon as he left, before he could change his mind, I took her to the Greyhound Station, bought her a ticket, and gave her all the money I had. I scribbled my name and number on a torn off piece of paper, telling her to call me if she ever needed anything or found herself in trouble. Jonathan didn't know I gave her my name, phone number, and money, and I prayed he wouldn't find out. When her bus pulled out of the station, I had 24 hours to make up all that money to give to Jonathan when he returned the next day.

Because of this girl, I found a little bit of hope. She doesn't know it, but in letting me help her get out of there, she helped me find the inspiration I needed to persevere through this life a little bit longer. She gave me a glimmer of hope for myself, my unborn daughter, and my family. She fueled my will to survive a little bit longer. Although I didn't have time or energy to dream about a future I didn't think I would live to see, helping her sparked another desire inside of me: that someday, if I got out, I may be able to help others stuck in "The Life."

One night, after five months of working for Jonathan and over halfway through my pregnancy, I woke up and knew something was terribly wrong. I called Jonathan and tried to convince him to take me to the hospital. His response still rings in my ears today, "I'm with Erika right now trying to sleep, and my tooth hurts. Stop bothering me." It seemed almost impossible to get him out of bed with another girl, but I insisted it was an emergency, so he finally did.

At the hospital, I gave birth to my stillborn daughter. The doctor blamed it on a bladder infection and the exhausted state of my body. A nurse asked me a few questions: what my address was, who the father was, and what my plans were. I could hardly answer any of her questions. I didn't have an address to give. I was terrified of the father. My plans were to survive. The hospital staff had seen women like me before. I seemed to them like just another strung-out prostitute who lost a child to "The Life." They didn't see the red flags. And I didn't reach out for help. Who could I trust? It seemed like everyone I met was judging me or was somehow involved with my trafficker. I had met corrupt doctors, lawyers, and law enforcement agents involved in this crime. The last thing I wanted to do was show my cards. And they didn't see the girl inside me, crying out for help and rescue. That day, I lost my child, was released from the hospital, and went back to work, even more broken-hearted than before. During my pregnancy, I was motivated to hold on, to stay alive, to survive. Now, my life had lost all meaning.

There are many dangers women have to navigate in "The Life." While traffickers are the most obvious, the tricks are also a problem. Traffickers are motivated to keep their victims somewhat safe so they can continue to get the one thing traffickers value: money. As long as you were making money and not breaking any rules, you would survive. Tricks, on the other hand, had nothing to lose. A trick could be anyone, no matter the age, race, occupation. Tricks can be doctors, lawyers, construction workers, law enforcement, unemployed, programmers, oil field workers— anyone. Not all tricks are violent. But no matter how they act, the bottom line is this: sex trafficking is a business of supply and demand. If people didn't want to buy sex (demand), there wouldn't be a need to enslave and exploit victims (the supply), because there would be no profit.

Although there are many reasons people purchase sex—addiction, loneliness, boredom, stress relief—two of them are the scariest. First, some tricks are motivated by power and control. They purchase sex for the experience of exerting complete control over someone. Second, some tricks are motivated by the desire to do certain acts that a sexual partner would never consent to. Often times these desires are motivated by violent material viewed on pornography.

One of the tricks I will never forget was an overweight, middle-aged, card-carrying sex offender. He was clearly mentally unstable. How did I know that? He showed up to the hotel room with gallons of bleach. I didn't want to let him in, for fear of what he was planning to do to me, but I had to. Hesitantly, I let the trick in the room, and he spoke to me in a very authoritative and demanding tone. It made me think of a "Criminal Minds" episode about an online child predator. The trick took a bleach bath before violently raping me. He then made me get in a bleach bath too. Afterwards, he silently walked out the door.

We would get many outcalls, and one night, Jonathan made another girl and me go to a call that turned from average to highly dangerous. The call was to service two tricks that were rooming together in a house. Upon arrival, it was clear they were high on drugs. They had requested and paid for an hour.

After two hours passed by, our trafficker called us to ask what was taking so long. Irritated, he told us to hurry up, charge them for the extra hour, and then leave. As the other girl and I attempted to make our way to the front door, one of the tricks pulled a gun on us and took our IDs and phone. He got up and barricaded the front door, holding us hostage. Our trafficker and the trick yelled at each other on the phone for a while, but to no avail. The other girl and I were forced to continue servicing the two tricks at gunpoint for hours into the night. Eventually, the girl and I escaped, leaving our IDs there. The next day, one of the tricks called us and apologized. They left our IDs on the front porch of their house the next day so we could get them.

On another occasion, we received an outcall where the trick wanted a "two-for-one special." When we got to the apartment, the trick paid for two hours, expecting each of us to service him for an hour. The other girl serviced him first, and I was to be second. As time passed, I sat outside the room waiting to be raped. Suddenly, the girl called me into the room they were in. She was trying to signal to me for help. I wasn't sure what was happening, but the trick was really angry and waving a knife around. He was saying that he wasn't happy with the service and wanted more. The girl had tried to say no to different services the man wanted that she didn't want to do. The man was angry because he had paid for her, and for the time they were spending together. He felt he should get whatever he wanted because he paid for her. In his mind, she was just like a product you buy at the store. The trick demanded his money back, but it had been over an hour and Jonathan had a no-refund policy. He told the trick this over the phone, which made the trick even angrier. I tried to calmly motion for the girl to walk towards me and run for the car. I was able to get between the trick and the other girl. The trick started threatening to kill us if he didn't get his money back. I threw the keys to the girl and told her to run and lock herself in the car. Meanwhile, I tried to make my way to the car while defusing the problem. The trick followed me outside and said if he didn't get his money back he would stab us both to death. I ended up giving him the money back and running, my instincts telling me that was the way to survive. Jonathan was furious with us for giving the money back. We had to work twice as hard that night to make up the lost money and time.

One of the scariest moments happened on an incall when I was expecting a trick to show up for a date. Jonathan was mad at me because I hadn't been able to answer many calls that night. Someone called my ad in the middle of the night and said he wanted to see me. The trick said he was on his way, but he still hadn't showed. I asked where he was and received no response. About five minutes later, he called me and said that he was standing outside in the parking lot waiting for me. He said he was going to kidnap, torture, and rape me, then slit my throat because I am a "dirty whore." He sounded like a serial killer and was talking in a really creepy voice. I hung up the phone and my trafficker messaged me saying I still had to see the trick. I didn't leave the room. About twenty minutes later, I heard the trick trying to pick the lock on my door. When he couldn't do that, he tried to break the door down. The trick called saying he was going to get inside, and I couldn't keep him locked outside forever. As this was happening, I tried to escape out the back door, but the trick must have heard me and run around the back to block me. This continued for quite some time, and then suddenly, everything was silent. An hour passed by as I hid inside a kitchen cabinet. He texted me again saying that I was beautiful, he just wanted to see me, and he was still waiting for me outside.

People have asked me countless times the very question you may be asking right now: "Why didn't you just run away?" Unless you've been in my shoes, I can't fully explain to you all the reasons I surrendered to trafficking as my fate. But here's what I can tell you.

I was hopeless. What reason did I have to believe my life could really be good or worth something? My whole life, I'd experienced pain, abuse, rejection, loneliness, and depression. Yes, I had a family that cared about me, and I'd known safety and opportunity, but it always came with strings attached and never seemed like something I could really have and keep. And now? What possibilities were there? At least my traffickers cared if I lived or died.

I was desperate. My trafficker had my phone, ID, and money. I felt like I had nowhere else to go and no one to turn to. I had dropped out of school, and my only job history of the past few years was off-and-on stints with Whataburger. What else was I going to do to survive? Some girls are drawn in for the money. For me, "The Life" was always about survival.

I was traumatized. Like most victims of trafficking, I suffered what's called "complex trauma" all throughout my trafficking. Complex trauma, also known as Complex Post Traumatic Stress Disorder (C-PTSD) occurs when bad, painful events happen over and over and over, changing the way your brain works. A single event, like a car wreck, robbery, or breakup can be traumatic. More intense events can result in PTSD. Repeated traumatic events over a period of time can cause C-PTSD, and it's very common with trafficking victims. Constant fear, rape, beatings, and inability to escape are all traumas, and they add up. C-PTSD changes your perception of yourself and the world. Because of what had happened to me, I was constantly looking for threats, stressed and full of adrenaline, even in safe situations. I felt worthless and hopeless. I had nightmares. All I could think about was surviving. I worked so hard to survive; there was no room left to dream or plan a way out.

I was afraid for my life. It was do or die. Work or get beaten. Work or starve. Work or risk harm to my family. Work or be sold to another trafficker. For example, one time another pimp tried to recruit me in the parking lot of the motel where we were staying. He tried to find out if I was a renegade. When he later saw Jonathan, he accused me of reckless eyeballing and told my trafficker I had been making eye contact with him. In "The Life," you keep your eyes on the ground. If you make eye contact with another pimp, it means you are choosing up. It's a very dangerous move, as it threatens both the income and the pride of a pimp. I denied that I'd looked at him, but my trafficker attacked me and planned to sell me to this other pimp. I screamed and drew attention to the room and the other trafficker backed out and left. I was spared being sold, and I was relieved. I knew how to survive with my pimp, and the only thing worse than being with him was the unknown of being with someone else. In the past, I had built up the courage and tried to run away from my traffickers but was unsuccessful every time. One of my traffickers searched for me and later found me on the streets, where he beat me and yelled at me, and dared me to try and escape again. All hope of escape was violently squashed. That was the day I learned to never try and run away, to never risk the consequences of escape.

I was in love, or so I thought. This concept may be the hardest to understand for someone who hasn't been through it. Jonathan knew that my deepest desire was to find acceptance and love, to be with someone. He used that against me and promised me love and affection and a life with him to create my illusion of romance. He bought me gifts and sometimes treated me with tenderness. He mixed this "love" with threats and violence. This confusing combination of tenderness and abuse produces what's called "trauma bonding" in your brain. You may be more familiar with this in the context of domestic violence, or prisoners of war as studied in the "Stockholm Syndrome," but it's also a very real and powerful phenomenon in sex trafficking.

Why not call the police? Since getting out of "The Life," I've met some incredible law enforcement agents, including some who played a big part in my rescue and recovery. I have also grown to know and deeply respect several, and consider them friends. However, in my personal experience before being trafficked, cops had never been there for me. In "The Life," cops were definitely not seen as the good guys. Along with other respected and trusted community figures, such as lawyers and doctors, FBI agents and police officers, both undercover and in uniform, exploited me. Other times, someone would call the police on our hotel room. They'd show up and tell me there had been a complaint filed against the room I was staying in, and there was too much suspicious traffic going in and out. They'd give me a few minutes to pack up and clear out or they'd arrest me for trespassing. To them, I was another strung out prostitute causing problems, not a victim of trafficking needing help and rescue. Not once did they ask if I needed help or if I was being victimized.

In 2013, a year after losing my daughter, I caught a case (was arrested) in Alabama along with Jonathan. I had plenty of criminal involvement at that point, and I still wasn't self-identifying as a victim. Sometimes I stole basic necessities out of desperation, and sometimes my trafficker forced me to peel a trick (steal) when I didn't make my quota. Jonathan operated on Pimps Up, Hoes Down status. If the set quota wasn't made, then we had to keep working until it was. This time though, the charge was more serious. We were charged with human trafficking of the girl from Waco whom I had helped escape a year before.

It all happened so fast. I clearly remember the shrill ringing of the hotel room's telephone piercing the silence. A man on the other end identified himself as a federal law enforcement agent, warning us that the room was surrounded. He said we had ten seconds to open the door and get on the ground, or else the door would be broken down. If we weren't on the ground, we would be shot. Suddenly, there was a loud banging on the door. Moments later, I found myself with my face to the ground and hands up, with multiple guns directed at me. All I could hear was a voice shouting for me to slowly crawl towards them.

Federal law enforcement had tracked us down. I didn't even know there was a warrant out for Jonathan's and my arrest, so I was confused and overwhelmed, to say the least. It was time to learn to survive a new life: the jail life. I witnessed women fighting and brutally beating each other, corrupt guards and inmates dealing drugs and other items, and a hierarchy of survival similar to the streets. Various crimes and victimizations, including human trafficking, occurred within the very walls that were meant to stop them. One day after "chow time," someone shouted my name across the jail pod, and a guard opened my cell door. I was commanded to

JULIA AT A RUSSIAN ORPHANAGE

JULIA AT FAMILY CHRISTMAS

JULIA'S HIGH SCHOOL GRADUATION

JULIA IN "THE LIFE"

JULIA'S MUGSHOT AT HER ARREST

« Я ГОСПОДЬ БОГ ВАШ, КОТОРЫЙ ВЫВЕЛ ВАС ИЗ ЗЕМЛИ ЕГИПЕТСКОЙ, ЧТОБ ВЫ НЕ БЫЛИ ТАМ РАБАМИ,
И СОКРУШИЛ УЗЫ ЯРМА ВАШЕГО, И ПОВЕЛ ВАС С ПОДНЯТОЮ ГОЛОВОЮ. »

(RUSSIAN SYNODAL VERSION, PUBLIC DOMAIN)

« I AM THE LORD YOUR GOD...
I BROKE THE BARS OF YOUR YOKE AND ENABLED YOU TO WALK WITH HEADS HELD HIGH. »

LEVITICUS 26:13

grab my stuff and go with the officers. They gave me no explanation. The next thing I knew, I was placed in a police car with Jonathan, and we made the long trip to Waco, Texas, handcuffed side by side in the back seat of the cop car. This gave Jonathan plenty of time to fill my mind with lies and threats.

Back in Waco, we were processed and booked in jail. I was treated like a criminal. Although I was on the opposite side of the jail, Jonathan sent a message to me. I was walking along the hallway after being called to the front desk, and someone called my name. This stranger told me Jonathan wanted me to know he had eyes on me and to keep quiet. I wasn't even safe from Jonathan in jail. Jonathan had a family member who handled the money for him when it got over $10,000, because he was afraid that if he possessed over that amount he could be arrested for money laundering. This family member, who was in law enforcement, bailed us out of jail.

When we got out of jail, we moved in with another family member of Jonathan's in San Antonio. This woman claimed to be a devout Christian, saying "praise the Lord" often, and her apartment was decorated with crosses and Bibles and Christian sayings. She worked at a drug rehab center and was a former drug addict herself. He paid her to keep me there while he traveled. Jonathan gave her my phone to hold onto, and she kept it in her bedroom, where she had a drawer full of phones. I always imagined these belonged to other girls like me, whose phones he had confiscated to keep them in his control. She put on a good show sometimes, acting like a friend who wanted to help me. For a while, I got a real job at Church's Chicken down the street. One day, she offered me a ride to work. As we pulled up, she said, "You know Yuli, whenever you are done being Jonathan's little whore, let me know, and I can help you get on your feet until you are able to live independently." For fear of Jonathan finding out that I had upset her, I had to say, "Thank you. You are so kind. I will let you know." She pretended to not approve of the life we were living. But if she didn't get paid with the money Jonathan earned from selling me and his other girls, she turned hostile, threatening to kick us out. She didn't really care that we were getting raped, as long as she was getting paid. Jonathan even told me his mom had helped him recruit girls, offering them drugs and making them dependent on him so they would turn tricks. I didn't trust this "Christian woman" at all. She expected Jonathan and me to attend church with her. This left a bad taste in my mouth for Christianity.

This wasn't my first interaction with "religion." Growing up, I had been taught about God. I was taught that he loved us, but I always saw him as a far off, authoritative figure. My family was very involved at church, and I was expected to participate. I went to youth group, played in the bell choirs, played church piano solos, and sang in the church choir. But at that point in my life, I was just going through the motions.

Ryan's family was Catholic, although they weren't very public about their faith. At the same time, his dad would turn away while his son beat, raped, and abused me, and made me sleep in the trunk of his car at night. He turned away while his son treated me like a caged animal, but would then welcome his son with open arms as if he was doing nothing wrong. His dad treated me like dirt, ignoring me, as if I was invisible. His dad talked about me demeaningly in front of me as if I couldn't hear him. He would look at me, shake his head, and mutter cruel things underneath his breath.

Derrick's mom claimed to be a Christian as well. She would talk about Jesus and say "Praise the Lord" throughout the day. But when she saw what Derrick was doing to me—the abuse, the rape, the cruelty—she turned away as if nothing was happening. She would make excuses for her son saying he has had a hard life, and she is so proud of him for making it through so much. She would tell me how sweet I am, but would then call and threaten me and my family when I would try and run away from him. I wanted nothing to do with this "Christianity" I experienced or with this God they claimed to worship.

In 2014, after two and a half years with Jonathan, we were working in Lubbock. Our case from the Waco arrest in 2013 was still active, and we were out on bond. At that point, he had a few other girls that had joined the family and were working for him out of a hotel. One night we received an outcall, and he showed it to me on another girl's track phone. At this point, I had moved up in the ranks to the bottom. This position gave me some security and control, and it helped him to keep his hands clean as he made me set up the tricks for myself and the other girls until they learned how. He often traveled around to check in on his other "business ventures," and he trusted me with some responsibilities of keeping his business running, although he could take this position from me at any point. Many bottom girls use violence, threats, and yelling to get the girls under them to work. I wasn't like that. I drove girls around, posted ads, and sometimes collected money, because that's what I had to do. Overall, I was still myself, naturally mellow, easygoing, and sweet. At times, it got intense, but I wasn't the violent type, and I tried to treat others with respect.

Jonathan was not new to this business. He had trafficked girls for 20 years before he even met me.

Just like he knew how to control his victims, he knew how to spot an undercover cop and how to evade arrest. Before an outcall, we always asked for a photo of our trick. Like usual, Jonathan showed me the picture of a trick and asked if I thought he was vice (undercover cop). I could immediately tell that he was, but I said no. That night, I really didn't care what happened to me. I had lost everything. I had no one, not even my own baby girl. Maybe the cop would show up and actually be a trick. Maybe he'd show up and arrest us. That night, I didn't even care about survival. I just wanted to get away from Jonathan or die. He drove me and another girl to the call, and we were arrested for prostitution.

That night, something happened to me that had never happened before. For the first time, I was asked the question that could change everything.

5

RESCUED

"Are you not wanting to be here? Do you need help? Do you want to get away from him?" The investigators asked me these questions as if they truly wanted to help me.

Everything inside me was screaming "YES! I want out! Get me away from him!" But I said no. I thought back to the other times when I had tried to ask for help and no one listened or believed me. I worried that the girl with me would tell Jonathan what I said. I was scared. They walked away, and I thought I'd missed my chance.

Later, they separated us and asked again, giving me another chance to see they were serious about helping me. For some crazy reason, I told them the truth. I waited for them to accuse me of lying, but for the first time in four years of being trafficked, I wasn't treated like a bad guy. I was treated like a victim. I didn't know how to react or what to say. I felt a little spark of hope, but I still didn't trust them or their motives. I wasn't going to give them anything else. They booked and processed us, and then Jonathan got a message to me again, telling me to stay silent. And I did. If he could get a message to me through a stranger in jail, he could do anything. This reminded me what he was capable of. It reminded me who was really in control. I was truly powerless. That spark of hope went out again.

Jonathan had instructed me to check in with his uncle on a weekly basis while we were in jail. Before my arrest, his uncle had never shown any concern for me, but now he told me he loved me and was there for me. He even put a small allowance of money that Jonathan had profited by trafficking me on my books so I could buy what I wanted while I was in jail. Jonathan wrote me a romantic letter in jail, although it was filled with hints to stay quiet. I was confused. Who do I trust?

Detectives interviewed and questioned me. I said I wanted help, but then shut down when they asked me about myself or my trafficker. I knew better. Jonathan had cops in his family, he kept tabs on me in jail, he knew my every word and move. I had to stay quiet.

Kim Clark, a detective from Waco, Texas, came to interview me about my case there. I didn't tell her anything. The Lubbock cops decided to try again. They were persistent, which is exactly what I needed.

Without their belief in me, I would have slipped back into the same life, but probably wouldn't have survived much longer.

They told me about something called "human trafficking," and that they believed I was a victim of it. I knew about "The Life" and I knew what I'd been through, but I thought everyone saw me as a criminal. Therefore, I didn't understand and saw myself as a criminal and not a victim. I was confused. They told me they could help me get out of this lifestyle.

While I was in jail, a Lubbock organization called Voice of Hope came to visit me. They told me they help women like me who have been assaulted and trafficked. I was filled with doubts and shame about how I could be a victim of human trafficking. They helped me begin to slowly understand what happened to me. I didn't trust anyone, and hearing them talk about the detectives being trustworthy was hard to believe. But as they continued working with me, and as I continued to meet with the detectives, Voice of Hope helped me build a spark of trust that continued to grow stronger after each meeting. They helped me look toward the future.

Even then, through the chaos inside of me, I heard a voice inside that sounded different. For so long, the voice in my head called me worthless, hopeless, a burden, a criminal. But I now heard words that stirred hope inside me, stronger than ever. I thought about what Voice of Hope and the detectives told me. They cared and wanted to help me. They saw me for who I was: Julia, a human being with value. They wanted to help me and bring Jonathan to justice. They made me feel like they genuinely cared, so my walls started to fall. I took the leap of faith. I told them everything: how I got there, what happened and about all the threats that he had made. It took a lot of courage and strength for me to choose to trust law enforcement, but I did it, little by little. They helped get many of my charges dropped and advocated on my behalf to help others see me as a victim.

Because of my trafficking charges in Waco, I was transferred to the jail there. I was terrified, afraid I'd done the wrong thing in telling them the truth. But after meeting people there, the flickering hope that was sparked inside me in Lubbock was reignited and kept growing stronger.

So here I was, at a fork in the road. I knew it was time to make my choice.

The detective who had visited me twice in Lubbock was there, and I chose to open up more to her as she showed me she really cared and believed my story. Another anti-trafficking organization, called UnBound, came to offer me help. I will never forget the question Susan with UnBound asked me when she met me in jail: "What can I do for you? What do you need right now?" The more UnBound worked with me, the more confident and safer I felt in sharing more information with the detectives. They weren't trying to manipulate or control me. They didn't try to tell me what to do. They asked me what I wanted. They encouraged me to stand strong when I was feeling doubtful or hesitant in working with law enforcement. An attorney volunteered his time to help me understand what was happening with my charge. This whole experience was so new. I started believing people really saw me for who I was. I started believing there was hope for my future and that I really could get help.

My parents came down to Waco to see me. I later learned that, desperately searching for help, they had learned of UnBound and contacted them on my behalf. Before going to the jail, they met with Susan Peters, the National Director from UnBound. She told them about meeting me in jail. She told them she didn't see me as a criminal or monster, but as a beautiful girl who had been manipulated into a bad situation. She told them I was a victim, and there was help for me. She told them when she asked me what I needed, I asked her to pray for the other girls out there, so they could be rescued and find God. Through the years of chaos, turmoil, and hopelessness we'd experienced together, those were the words my parents needed to hear. My parents supported me while I was in jail, writing letters to me almost daily, sending cards, and putting money on my books. Despite everything, they still loved me and wanted me to be OK.

I am sure some of you reading this are wondering how I went from not wanting anything to do with Christianity to asking for prayers on behalf of other girls out there. This change of perspective certainly didn't happen overnight. In fact, I didn't start to consider God until nearing the end of my trafficking story. After losing my daughter, Yuliana, I wanted nothing to do with God. That was the nail that sealed the coffin for me. I didn't pray, I didn't think about God, and I didn't want to. Ever again. However, strange events began to unfold when Jonathan and I moved in with his family member in San Antonio. I didn't understand their significance at the time, but in hindsight, I understand completely.

One day Jonathan took us to see a lawyer in San Antonio. Neither of us knew this man. We were meeting him for the first time. However, I had a dream the night before Jonathan took us to visit him. In this dream, I saw the office we would be meeting this man in. The man was supposed to be alone. However, in my dream, the man had a business partner who appeared out of nowhere. As the dream continued, Jonathan talked to the men while I stood in the corner, watching from the shadows of a stairway. Jonathan and the men began to argue, and they grew louder and louder. Meanwhile,

I was wishing I knew how to get back home. In my dream, all I wanted to do was run out of the door, not looking back until I made it home. Suddenly, an angel appeared and was singing. It was really strange, but I had this feeling I should follow the angel. I followed the angel out of the office and down to a gate. The angel unlocked the gate without speaking, signaling to me that I was free. I flew through the gates and woke up. I didn't know what to make of this dream. The next day when we met the lawyer, I was stunned. I saw the office exactly as it had been in my dream. My dream was real, even down to the unannounced business partner appearing. I didn't think much else about God at the time. This was the first seed that was planted.

A week before I was arrested and ultimately freed, I had another dream that law enforcement had suddenly arrived at the hotel and whisked me away in the middle of the night to freedom. A week after having this dream, Jonathan and I were arrested in Lubbock, where I was ultimately freed from him and "The Life." After I was arrested, I began to have other dreams. It was surreal. God started speaking to me in dreams, and I didn't even realize it was God! Throughout this time, I slowly started considering God and Christianity again. I still wasn't fully convinced. It definitely took time. But as time passed, I slowly began to feel a connection with God, no matter how weak it was. I had some other strange encounters after this. Eventually, I even started a Bible study with my cellmates in the Waco jail. I was already a believer, but I had a yearning to learn more. That's when I met UnBound.

I was released from jail with an ankle monitor because I had a pending charge and because the police were concerned I'd run, and they'd lose track of me. Although they were probably right, I still hated wearing it. I tried to get it off, even scheming to put it on a dog until I could clear town. I wasn't successful. In "The Life," you become used to constantly running from place to place, especially when things get hard or trouble appears. The ankle monitor ensured that I didn't leave when things got tough. I had to stick it out and work through the challenges I faced in my healing. After a brief time staying with my parents, I spent a few months at Mosaic, a domestic violence and human trafficking shelter located in Dallas. There I began receiving case management, counseling, and other needed resources. Mosaic helped me get plugged into New Friends New Life, another anti-trafficking organization in Dallas. After a few months, UnBound helped me find Redeemed Ministries, an aftercare safehouse created to help human trafficking survivors heal in a therapeutic environment. For the first time in years, there was an option for me to truly find safety, healing, and a new life.

6

ROAD TO HEALING AND SURVIVORSHIP

Thank you for sticking with me as I've shared the hardest parts of my story. Now, I want to tell you about some of the wonderful things that have happened since I became a survivor of sex trafficking. For so long, my driving force was to survive in "The Life," but I was never truly out of danger, and I was forced into horrible situations to survive. Survival was a day-by-day struggle. After I was rescued, I went from fighting to survive to truly becoming a survivor. I did it. I survived. And now it was time to move on from that dark world.

I want you to know that the path to recovery is not easy, and it's not always a straight line toward healing. In my healing process, I have made poor choices and forgotten who I was from time to time. My life is complicated, and I still suffer the effects of my trauma and the lifestyle I was forced to live. I want to tell you about these challenges and how I'm taking them on with the advocates around me. But first, let me tell you about my life post-trafficking.

I went to Redeemed when I was 22 years old, after four years of being trafficked. Redeemed offers a holistic approach to address the physical, emotional, mental, and spiritual needs of survivors. There, I learned who I am as a survivor. I learned what genuine and unconditional love is. I learned how to love myself. I learned to let go of my trafficking brands, outwardly and inwardly. Outwardly, I had my trafficker's name tattooed on me, a constant reminder of the past I was trying to leave behind. At Redeemed, I was connected with pro-bono brand removals through Phoenix Charities, and now my tattoos are almost gone. I still have some sessions to go, but it won't be long until they are completely removed. Inwardly, I had many brands as well. I was branded internally with words: worthless, prostitute, bottom, depressed, failure, criminal, unlovable, abandoned, addict, property, and even victim. Through counseling, time, and a lot of hard work, those brands faded. In their place, I have new labels: *overcomer, survivor, leader, advocate, student, employee, daughter, sister, aunt, and friend.*

I learned healthy ways to cope with the loss, pain, and abuse I experienced because of trafficking, including the loss of my precious daughter. I received medical care, financial assistance, and counseling. I had a safe place to live, which allowed me to process life and get back on my feet.

Although that all sounds wonderful, it was a challenging process. It's not easy to dive into the most painful memories of your greatest abuse. By the time I was 22, I had been moved across the country, raped thousands of times, and arrested multiple times. That's a lot to process.

Everything inside you wants to use your old coping mechanisms for pain: running away, numbing with alcohol and drugs, and lashing out at others. A lot of survivors don't make it through recovery programs because of how challenging the process is. It's hard to voluntarily give up control of your life and let someone else help you make healthy decisions. For so long, I'd been forced to give up control and experienced others making decisions for me. But now, if I wanted to stay in the program, I had to choose to give up control and trust others, if I truly wanted a new life. I was so used to having to survive, making split-second decisions in moments of danger. Giving up control was really hard. Trusting that all my needs were going to be met consistently was extremely challenging. Giving up this control proved to be foundational in my healing and to helping me reach true survival.

There were many times when I was homesick and just wanted to be with my family but couldn't. I wanted to leave in the middle of the night and go stay with them. Many times, I wanted to call my family but had to wait until designated call days. This was also hard. It was hard to wait for a resident advisor to help us access email or apply for various things we needed, because we weren't allowed to have our own phones or computers. This was one of the hardest things because I was so used to having technology access all the time. These restrictions kept me from being contacted by past relationships who would try to suck me back into "The Life" when I was feeling weak. Not being allowed to listen to "Zero" and "Pimp C" was tough. I didn't understand why our music couldn't be our own. Slowly, over time, I learned to appreciate other rap artists who focused on messages of hope and positive content, instead of those who rapped about treating women as objects for sex. I was used to being constantly on the go. At Redeemed, I wasn't constantly on the go. There were many times when I had to learn to just be still and learn how to relax and take care of myself. All these challenges were milestones that I accomplished on my journey of healing.

I learned that God is not just an "authoritative" God, but a loving and relational one. God doesn't care only about obedience. He wants to have a genuine relationship with me. While I still grapple with understanding God and why evil things were allowed to happen to me, I also have learned that I am a daughter in Christ and that it was bad people, not a bad god, who caused me so much pain. I learned that God takes these awful things that happen to us and turns them into something good, but only if I let Him do that. I chose to be re-baptized while I was at Redeemed. It was an amazing feeling, being re-baptized and feeling the water wash away my past. Embracing this program and fighting for healing ultimately gave me back the control that had been stolen from me years before.

By the grace of God, and not without some issues, I successfully completed the program in 2015. I cannot thank the amazing, selfless staff at Redeemed enough for helping me get my life back. I did so well that they offered me a job on their staff. I decided instead I wanted to experience the freedom of living my own life for the first time and being closer to family. I chose to go back to DFW to a transitional program. It ended up being a bad experience. No program is perfect, and even when people have good intentions, they don't always handle situations well. Some hurtful things happened while I was there, and I made the bad decision to move out with a guy I met. I was and still am in the process of learning how to have healthy conflict and build healthy relationships, and sometimes we make mistakes even when headed in the right direction. I quickly realized that moving in with this guy was a bad decision, and with some help, I moved out to live on my own. I am proud of myself for recognizing this time that even though I'd gotten into a bad relationship, I was worth more than that and could get out.

7

FINDING HOPE IN PRESENT DAY

Today, I'm reunited with my family and living in a stable environment. My family and I are closer now than we have ever been before. We do things together and talk regularly. While there is still room to grow, we have begun reconciling our past differences with one another.

In the fall of 2016, my Waco trafficking charge was dropped, and I have an even brighter future ahead of me. My last trafficker, Jonathan, was convicted and sentenced to 40 years in prison on another charge. Before Jonathan had taken a plea bargain, I had received a call from a Waco district attorney letting me know I may need to travel to Waco and testify against him. The thought of having to face him in court was very scary and made me extremely nervous. I was terrified of having to look at him in court, tell of the abuses I and many others suffered, and openly tell the court of his crimes. I was fearful of Jonathan and what he would do to me and my family if I did this. I also wasn't sure if I could get through the process of testifying against him, while having to relive the traumas I experienced by his hand. Ultimately, I didn't have to testify, as Jonathan took a plea bargain instead of taking his case to trial. One of these days, I may have to face him to press my own charges. If that day comes, I'll be ready.

You may be wondering what happened to the others. For mine and my family's safety, I didn't use their real names in this story. Ryan seems to be worse off than before. He has kids now, and has become very public on Facebook, parading his guns around and publicizing his threats and hatred of people. Derrick was arrested at least a couple of other times for failure to ID and family assault. Charles is probably out and about somewhere. Last I saw him was in Arlington. I never knew his real name, so knowing where he is or if he is still trafficking people is impossible to determine. He showed nothing but coldness to me, so I can imagine he is still trafficking and abusing other people unless he has since been arrested.

I've been blessed with jobs that allow me to help people and make a difference. Over the past few years, I have volunteered with and consulted for UnBound. In 2017, I started working on staff with UnBound Fort

Worth, already seeing my dream of helping others become a reality.

I am excited to be working as a Survivor Leader and UnBound Fort Worth's Survivor Advocacy Coordinator. I work for an amazing boss who is compassionate and dedicated to advocating for both her employees and clients. Her passion in helping victims and survivors shines through her work. I am blessed to work alongside a team of advocates, where we operate a 24-hour hotline. When we receive a hotline call, one of us goes out and meets the client wherever she or he is located, focusing on building rapport and a relationship with the client. Working for one of the organizations that has walked with me from the beginning of my survivorship journey is incredible. I also worked for a short time for Redeemed Ministries as a Resident Advisor in their safe house. It has been such a joy and privilege being able to work alongside this special group of people that saw the literal worst and best of me, unconditionally loving and supporting me throughout my struggles and achievements. I couldn't think of a better setup than working for UnBound and Redeemed, people who I am honored to consider family.

I completed my Associates Degree in 2018 and am working toward my dual Bachelor's in Social Work and Criminal Justice to become better equipped to help victims of sex trafficking. I know that with my experience and my education, I can help victims transition into survivors and then into leaders, just as I have. I can share with them some of the hope that was once shared with me, reminding them that they are not alone.

I have had some amazing opportunities since being rescued from trafficking, and I know this is just the beginning. I've shared my story in front of large audiences, helping them understand that trafficking is real and there is hope, if we all work together. I've testified in front of state legislators, advocating for laws to be changed to better protect and support trafficking victims. I've consulted with groups of law enforcement and service providers, bringing a survivor's perspective to their work. I've had the opportunity and honor to meet with and mentor other survivors. I've sat across from victims and told them there is a way out.

Collaboration has been central to my story of freedom and restoration. Without all of the individuals, organizations, and different agencies working with one another to advocate on my behalf and meet all of my needs, I would not be where I am today. Victims of sex trafficking, like me, need a lot of support to empower them to become survivors. One individual or entity alone cannot help meet every need. Each individual and entity has its own skill set that benefits us in our journeys of healing. Everyone—a friend, a mentor, a detective, a donor—is a critical piece in solving the puzzle. With everyone working together for the common good of the survivor, healing and restoration can be accomplished. I am grateful that I get to demonstrate that through my story.

As I mentioned, I still face challenges and roadblocks that I struggle with today because of my trafficking. I have health challenges. I still need counseling to work through my Complex Post Traumatic Stress Disorder (C-PTSD), flashbacks, nightmares, and triggers due to the poly-victimization and complex trauma I have endured. I want to learn how to better trust people and to continue to have and maintain healthy relationships and boundaries. I have thousands of painful memories—rape, violence, and loss—that can never be erased. I have to work hard to improve my really bad credit score. I still have a criminal record that presents challenges. I have a charge that has not been expunged and shows up on my record when I apply for jobs or housing. I'm even barred from some scholarships. I have to fight harder to have doors open for me. I have to face those who still place labels and cast judgments on me because of my past. But I am free. I am safe. I am sober. No one is telling me what to do. I get to earn, spend, and save my money on my own terms. I have real friendships and relationships. No one is beating me or threatening me. I am incredibly relieved that I never have to sell my body again. My body is my own. I am pursuing my dreams. I am proving that a victim of sex trafficking can get out of "The Life," stay out of "The Life," and thrive. I truly have survived "The Life."

I am determined, and I have support, and I will overcome any obstacles one by one, making a way for others. I am restored, and I am a survivor. You can be too.

AFTERWORD

UnBound frequently receives calls from mothers desperate to find help for their daughters who are being trafficked or at high risk of victimization. As a mother of four daughters myself, these calls often bring me to tears, as I hear the heartbreak, fear, and desperation driving family members to reach out to us. Calls like these fuel the fire that drives us to keep doing what we do.

One day, we received a different kind of call. I heard the voice of a mom, familiar in its desperation and grief, but telling me the story of her daughter sitting in jail a few miles from our office. This story rang a bell for me as I connected this mother's story to the story on the front page of our local newspaper. Police had just arrested a male and female accused of trafficking a runaway girl from a local youth home. Knowing this would be a whole different kind of case, I set up a conference call between a local attorney who volunteers his services, the mother, and me to figure out next steps.

When I visited Julia in jail, I was immediately impressed by her gentleness and concern for others being forced into the world of sex trafficking. Although she had no reason to trust me, she was responsive to our offer of help. Because of her involvement in this case, it took some time and effort to demonstrate to authorities that she had been forced into this crime. The real criminal was her trafficker and she was another one of his victims. I vividly remember the day Julia was transferred to an aftercare home from the local jail. Her parents came to my office to pick up some clothes for Julia before they went to see her one more time before she left. I told them they had a beautiful, intelligent daughter. I told them that when I asked her how our team could pray for her, she asked us to pray "that the other girls will get rescued and find God." Her parents looked at me in shock and disbelief. They were so relieved that I didn't see Julia as a monster, a prostitute, or a trafficker, but as the woman she truly could be. The second they left, I rushed back to my office as I burst into tears.

What would happen if organizations like UnBound and the many others who have walked with Julia were not there? We have the opportunity to see past the ugly scabs and scars of trauma and survival and look into the eyes of each human being seeing the dignity inside—the image of God. This book is an invitation for you to come face to face with the horrible realities of human trafficking and to choose not to look away. It is an invitation to join the fight.

UnBound began in 2012, born out of my exposure to great exploitation as I traveled around the world with Antioch Ministries International. I learned that there are more than 35 million modern day slaves in our world today. I heard the stories of victims of sex trafficking, both male and female, and I knew we had to do something. I felt that the Church needed to be activated to play our part.

UnBound's mission is to mobilize the church and activate local communities to fight human trafficking. Initially we envisioned our work would focus on international human trafficking but as we researched, our team learned that sex trafficking is happening right here at home in our own communities. We have since started chapters to fight human trafficking in several U.S. cities as well as in Mongolia and Cambodia, and we're growing all the time. We have trained thousands of professionals, community members, and youth. We have had the honor to serve hundreds of brave victims and survivors, and have stories of victories, discouragements, breakthrough, pain, and restoration. And we know we are just a drop in the bucket. We stand alongside thousands of organizations, joining arms to fight.

In these pages, you read of Julia's great pain, disappointment, abuse, and broken dreams. Can you imagine writing out the most painful experiences of your life to share with the world? Good thing the story does not end there. You also read of freedom, justice, redemption, vision, and purpose. I hope you finished the last page inspired by Julia's resilient courage and motivated to join the fight to end human trafficking. Use your voice, your influence, your resources to make a difference. The Julias of the world are worth it.

We are thrilled that Julia is now part of our team, serving others and giving critical input into the work we do to combat slavery and ignite hope.

Proverbs 29:7 says, "The righteous care about the justice for the poor, but the wicked have no such concern." I am so thankful for our church and many community partners that care about the injustice of modern day slavery and are doing all they can to rescue and restore those that are entrapped. I would not want to be named among the *wicked* that have no concern. Thank you for reading Julia's story. I hope you will join us in combating slavery and igniting hope.

SUSAN PETERS
National Director, UnBound

COULD YOU BE A VICTIM OF HUMAN TRAFFICKING?

It can be really hard to admit that you may be a victim. It was for me, at least. But admitting that I was a victim helped me in a lot of ways. First, it helped me to let go of "The Life." For so long, I blamed myself for the life I was stuck in, which made me feel like there was no other option. When I realized I was a victim, my desire grew to fight back and get out. Second, it helped me to access help. It's really hard and humbling to let go of your fight for survival and let others help you fight. Realizing that I was a victim helped me let down my walls, stop fighting so hard, and start trusting other people to help me heal. Whether you need help to stop drug use, have tattoos removed, find counseling, build healthy relationships, learn a job skill, or find a safe place to live, there is a lot of help out there, and a lot of people who want to help.

Now I'm no longer a victim. Because I accessed that help, I've become a survivor and a leader who can stay free and use my voice to bring that freedom to others. I believe you can do the same.

> Is someone making you work by use of threats, manipulation, or violence?
>
> Does someone else have possession of your ID, money, or bank account?
>
> Are you free to come and go as you wish?
>
> Are you unpaid or paid very little for your work? Is someone else taking the money that you make?
>
> Are you involved in prostitution, stripping, or the making of pornography?
>
> Do you have a pimp or other person managing or controlling your work?
>
> Are you under 18 and involved in the commercial sex industry?

If you suspect you are a victim of human trafficking, please reach out for help.

National Resources

In case of an emergency, always call 911.

National Human Trafficking Hotline

This hotline is 24/7, anonymous, and multilingual. They can help you figure out what your next steps are and connect you to the best resources in your area.
Call: 1-888-373-7888
Text: "BEFREE" to 233733

Local Resources

- Domestic Violence Shelters
- Crime Victim Advocacy Centers
- Human Trafficking Advocacy Groups
- Police Department Victim Services

Julia's Resources

UnBound (Locations across the United States)
UnBoundnow.org

Mosaic Family Services (Dallas, Texas)
MosaicServices.org
Hotline: 214-823-4434

Redeemed Ministries (Texas)
RedeemedMinistries.com

New Friends New Life (Dallas, Texas)
NewFriendsNewLife.org
214-965-0935

Voice of Hope (Lubbock, Texas)
VoiceofHopeLubbock.org
Hotline: 806-763-RAPE (7273)

COULD YOU RECOGNIZE
HUMAN TRAFFICKING?

Anyone can be part of the fight against human trafficking if you know what to look for. Below is a list of red flags that could indicate human trafficking. Although many of these red flags could have other explanations, if you suspect trafficking, trust your instincts and make a report.

The Basics: If a person has been forced, tricked, or manipulated to provide labor or commercial sex, he or she is a victim of human trafficking. If someone under the age of 18 is providing commercial sex, he or she is a victim of human trafficking.

For Community Members:

(Resource from UnBound, **UnBoundnow.org**)

WHAT TO LOOK FOR

- Malnourished/in bad health
- With an older, controlling person
- Older boyfriend and friends
- Limited/no access to money, ID, or visa
- Has a manager/pimp
- Sudden change of behavior
- Branding, tattoos, bruises, scars
- Runaway, homeless, truant
- Recruited through false promises
- Won't make eye contact
- Drug addiction and STIs
- Involved in commercial sex

Hotel Industry:

WHAT TO LOOK FOR

- Room with multiple people going in and out
- Rooms rented at hourly rate or extended stay
- Multiple women or younger girls that seem unrelated
- Signs of control or constant observation of potential victims
- Pays with cash or prepaid card

Teachers and School Personnel:

WHAT TO LOOK FOR

- Much older boyfriend/friends
- Anxious, fearful or submissive behavior
- Abrupt change in behavior, school attendance, or attention to schoolwork
- Shows signs of depression, PTSD, or suicidal ideation
- History of running away from home or foster care placements
- Shows signs of malnutrition, chronic fatigue, or dehydration
- Sudden influx of income, materials, or clothing

Parents or Care Givers:

WHAT TO LOOK FOR

- Drug or alcohol use
- Older boyfriend or friend group
- Decline in school grades and attendance
- Sudden influx of income, materials, or clothing
- Unsupervised or deceptive use of social media and messaging apps
- Dressing inappropriately
- Sexting or having sex with multiple partners

Healthcare Workers:

WHAT TO LOOK FOR

- Chaperone who speaks for patient or seems overly involved
- Disorientation or inability to answer simple questions
- Little or no money or ID
- Substance abuse/psychiatric complaints
- STIs, infectious diseases, evidence of little medical care
- Signs of physical and/or sexual abuse
- Suspicious branding or tattoos
- Gut feeling

Like Julia, most victims will not self-identify. Make sure the patient feels safe and is alone and ask specific, non-judgmental questions.

WHAT TO DO

- Do NOT put yourself or the victim in danger by confronting a suspected victim, buyer, or trafficker.
- Document your observations of physical details of all parties including cars, clothes, tattoos, and physical features, as well as reasons for suspected trafficking.
- Call the National Human Trafficking Hotline to share whatever information you collected. Call 1-888-373-7888 or text "INFO" to 233733.

For Law Enforcement:

WHAT TO LOOK FOR

- Signs of injury, fatigue, undernourishment
- Unkempt or provocative clothing
- Acts intimidated or frightened of the person they are with or the driver in car
- Lack of eye contact or eye contact with law enforcement
- Unable to provide explanations or simple answers, unsure of current location
- Does not have personal identification in possession
- Refers to driver as "boyfriend," "girlfriend," or other relation, with little detailed information about them
- Tattoos or branding indicating possession
- Living on the premises/inside the business or transported to work by employer or business
- Unable to state their wages when asked; lack of paychecks or evidence of payments to employees
- Does not speak English and/or appears unaware of surroundings
- Employer abusive to employees (verbal or physical)
- Surveillance cameras located in uncommon places of the business

IMMEDIATE RESPONSE

- Secure evidence appropriately (phones, photos, IDs, money, drugs, etc.).
- Separate all persons to avoid coached answers
- Ask detailed questions and look for conflicting information
- Ask for origins of tattoos and/or injuries
- Collect all phone numbers
- Detail all information from incident in field interview report to corroborate future investigations
- Contact federal and local law enforcement to report incident, especially if an arrest is made
- Recognize potential victims may resist or appear uncooperative because of fear or trauma

The victim's safety is the #1 priority. Get victim to a safe location away from perpetrator and other suspects. Involve victim service provider or advocacy agency as soon as possible.

BUILDING RAPPORT

- Ask him or her what name he or she would like to be called. Call the victim by his or her requested name; don't call him or her a "victim," "prostitute," or any other labels or names.
- If you're not familiar with terminology or street concepts mentioned by victim, ask for an explanation. Don't guess.

- Never make assumptions; always ask for clarification.
- Never ask "Why?" (ex. "Why did you do/say that?" "Why didn't you run away?" etc.) If a "why" question is needed for investigation, consider phrasing these questions in a less accusing way. (ex. "What made you feel like you needed to stay?" or "What led you to believe he was telling the truth?" "What was going on when that happened?")
- Always knock on the door and ask the victim if it is alright to step inside before entering into a room where a victim is located.
- Upon entering a room where a victim is, ask the victim where he or she would like you to sit. Allow the victim to face and/or sit by an exit when possible
- Don't assume the victim resents their trafficker; often times the victim will have a trauma-bond with the trafficker and will believe he or she is in love with him (her "boyfriend").
- If the victim has visible tattoos, ask about them in a neutral, non-judgmental way to discover if they may be brands.
- Provide at least two *options* to give a victim a sense of safety and control. The feeling of being cornered or controlled may drive a victim to be uncooperative.

- Try to make the victim more comfortable by asking if he or she would like a blanket or something to eat or drink. If possible, conduct interviews when a victim is well-rested and sober.
- When talking with a victim, try to be at eye level, instead of standing or towering over him or her. This helps the victim feel less intimidated and afraid.
- Never assume it is alright to touch a victim (ex. patting on the back, hugging, etc.).
- Let the victim know what is about to happen beforehand, especially when it will involve a transition from one place to another or when you will next communicate. This will help him or her feel less on-edge if he or she has an idea of what is coming.
- When talking with a victim, make sure to have a soft tone. If your tone is loud and/or deep, it could come across as intimidation.

(Resource from Heart of Texas Human Trafficking Coalition, **hothtc.org**)

Thank you for doing your part to fight human trafficking and offer help to victims!

ABOUT THE AUTHOR

JULIA WALSH is a Survivor Leader in the fight against sex trafficking. She is passionate about empowering other survivors as a consultant, speaker, mentor, and advocate. Adopted from a Russian orphanage as a baby, Julia struggled to adjust in her North Texas home. When she left for college in 2010, she quickly fell victim to the dark world of domestic violence, drugs, and sex trafficking.

After four years in "The Life," Julia was rescued and began her road to survivorship. Julia now works at UnBound Fort Worth as the Survivor Advocacy Coordinator, collaborating with law enforcement and victim service providers to support human trafficking survivors in Tarrant County. In her spare time, Julia continues to pursue a Dual Bachelor's degree in Social Work and Criminal Justice, while also speaking at human trafficking conferences around the country and advocating for policy change on behalf of survivors like her.

ABOUT UNBOUND

UnBound is mobilizing the Church and activating local communities to fight human trafficking through prevention, professional training, and survivor advocacy.

Founded in 2012 in Waco, Texas, UnBound has expanded into an international network of chapters, combating slavery and igniting hope in communities across the United States and around the world. UnBound educates and empowers youth, spreads awareness through outreach and training, equips professionals to identify victims, advocates for human trafficking survivors, and activates local communities to collaborate in the fight against human trafficking.

UnBound's outreach, education, and training has reached tens of thousands worldwide, with an ever-increasing reach. As awareness grows, so does identification. UnBound has served more than 100 human trafficking survivors, with an increasing number every year.

UnBound

For more information on UnBound,
visit **UnBoundnow.org**.

A NOTE ON THE TYPE

This book was set in Chronicle Text, a "blended Scotch" typeface. A vigorous hybrid of time-honored forms and contemporary design strategies, Chronicle Text is a new suite of high-performance text faces that brings strength and utility to the classic serif. Available from Hoefler & Co., New York.

Typeset by Nord Compo,
Villeneuve-d'Ascq, France

Printed and bound by Bethany Press International,
Bloomington, Minnesota